Praise for *Going It Alone*

I wish this book had existed when I first went independent. It would have saved me from a lot of mistakes. Even now, twenty years after first going independent, I learned a few things. Each chapter in Karl Wiegers's *Going It Alone* is full of powerful advice, most of it from Wiegers himself. But he's also wisely included chapters from experts on specific topics. If you are a newly independent consultant or are contemplating it, *Going It Alone* has the advice you need to succeed.

—*Mike Cohn, Co-founder of the Scrum Alliance and the Agile Alliance*

I've looked to Karl Wiegers for business guidance for many years, and I'm thrilled to see him share these ideas in this interesting, practical, and to-the-point book. Many consulting books are a bit ho-hum to read, but this one kept me turning the pages. I'm not an independent consultant, but this book's breadth of topics reaches well beyond that audience. Whether you are a consultant, business owner, aspiring leader inside a professional services organization, or budding author, you will find value here.

—*Joy Beatty, Vice President of Research and Development at Seilevel*

I've read most of the consulting books recommended in *Going It Alone*, and they are all as good as suggested. What makes *Going It Alone* stand out from the others is that Karl Wiegers and his colleagues easily cover the broadest landscape of issues that you may encounter as a consultant and provide practical, down-to-earth advice to navigate these issues. Even after consulting for fifteen years, I picked up a handful of valuable tips for future use!

—*Jim Brosseau, Clarrus Consulting Group*

This book captures in a very readable way a collection of lessons learned from Karl's years of experience and from the experience of others. I find two of the techniques described here to be especially helpful—not only to novices, but to those of us who've been doing independent consulting for decades. The first is the use of checklists, a simple but very effective way to avoid mistakes. The second is a collection of business rules (or policies, as he also names them), a pithy collection of lessons you won't have to learn the hard way. In addition to these two notions, there is a wide range of other advice on topics that will help make you a successful speaker, advisor, and author—enjoy!

—*Dr. Joyce Statz, Independent Consultant in Business Analysis and Process Improvement*

A singularly lucid and entertaining guide to the full lifecycle of working as an indie consultant. No one considering leaving the dark side of corporate employment should make the jump until they have read this book—twice. It will save you unimaginable grief.

—Gary K. Evans, Agile Coach and Use Case Expert

Simply put, this is the book I wish I'd had available to me when I started consulting. I had never had to market my services, bid against competitors, incorporate my business, negotiate deals with partners and clients, or protect my intellectual property. I learned the hard way. *Going It Alone* distills those hard-earned lessons so you don't have to. It took me years to figure out how to leverage my work through passive income; Karl devotes a large section to it. It almost seems unfair: he lets the reader in on the secrets that took the rest of us a lot of pain to learn. The book provides valuable advice on pretty well everything that touches on the consultant's life, from how to work with partners, to what to cover in contracts, to the more philosophical questions of consulting like balancing life and work. If you're starting out on your own, you couldn't do yourself a better favor than reading this book.

—Howard Podeswa, CEO Noble Inc., author of The Business Analyst's Handbook

Going It Alone

Essential Tips for the Independent Consultant

Karl Wiegers

Agent Q Bookworks
Happy Valley, Oregon

Going It Alone: Essential Tips for the Independent Consultant

Copyright © 2018 Karl Wiegers
Published in the United States by Agent Q Bookworks, an imprint of Process Impact

All rights reserved. No part of this publication may be reproduced, distributed, or transmitted in any form or by any means, or stored in a database or retrieval system, without the prior written permission of the publisher of this book, except in the case of brief quotations embodied in critical reviews. For information contact:

Agent Q Bookworks
11491 SE 119th Drive
Happy Valley, OR 97086-8278

ISBN: 978-0-9992053-3-4

Printed in the United States of America

*For Chris, who ate countless dinners
alone during all those years when
I was a road warrior*

Contents

Introduction 1
    How I got here 1
    Being self-employed 2
    Casting a large net for knowledge 3
    How the book is organized 4
    Some caveats 6
    Why to keep reading 6

Part 1 Setting Up Shop 7

Chapter 1 Hanging Out the Shingle 9
    Choose a good name 10
    Go online 11
    Draw a crowd 12
    Share what you know 12
    Get on stage 13
    It all adds up 13

Chapter 2 Hey, World, Here I Am! 15
    Marketing you! 16
    Dealing with third-party placement 17

Chapter 3 Modes of Consulting: What's Your Preference? 19
    Outside looking in 19
    Many hands make light work 23
    Teamwork 25

Chapter 4 The Consulting Lifestyle 29
    Why be a consultant? 29
    It's a family business 31
    Working with family members 33

Part 2 On the Job 35

Chapter 5 Make a List, Check It Twice 37

Chapter 6 No Easy Answers 41

Chapter 7 Consultants as Legitimate Leaders: The Goldilocks Approach 45
    Too weak 46
    Too strong 47

Just right 47

Chapter 8 OMG, What Have I Done?! Anticipating Risks When Working with Others 49
    Clients 52
    Business partners 52
    Collaborators 52

Chapter 9 The Dream Client 55

Chapter 10 Clients Who Give You Grief 59
    Getting stiffed 59
    Firing a client 61
    Questionable ethics 62
    A poor fit 63
    Knocking your head against the wall 63
    Clients who go dark 64

Chapter 11 Difficult Client? Try these Quick Tips 65

Chapter 12 The Challenges and Adjustments of Remote Consulting 69
    Facing the challenges 70
    Five strategies for mastering remote engagement 71
    Collaboration tools 74
    Fulfilling the consulting promise 74

Part 3 Practicalities 75

Chapter 13 What Are You Worth? 77
    Happy either way 77
    What the market will bear 78
    You want fries with that? 80

Chapter 14 Money Matters for the New Consultant 81
    First, hire an accountant 81
    Rates: Don't be a cheap date 82
    Don't burn cash on an office 85
    Sole proprietorship versus incorporation 85
    Planning for retirement 86

Chapter 15 Get It In Writing 87
    Speaking agreement 87
    Consulting agreements 89
    Courseware licensing agreement 89
    The usual disclaimer 90

Chapter 16 Everything's Negotiable 91
    Fees 92
    Cancellation 92
    Usage rights 93
    Video recording 94

    Insurance 94
    Other expenses 95
Chapter 17 **It's a Matter of Policy** 97
    On traveling 97
    On finances 101
    On client relations 103
Chapter 18 **For Your Protection** 107
    Business liability 107
    Business property 108
    Professional liability 108
    Life 109
    Health care 110
    Disability income 111
    A useful tip 112

Part 4 Building the Business 113

Chapter 19 A Kind of Business Plan 115
    Income while you sleep #1: Book royalties 116
    Income while you sleep #2: Licensing 116
    Income while you sleep #3: E-learning courseware 118
    Income while you sleep #4: E-books 119
    Income while you sleep #5: Other products 120
    Income while you sleep #6: Affiliate programs 120
Chapter 20 Be Prepared for the Unexpected 123
Chapter 21 How to Get Repeat Business from Your Clients 127
    Applying systems thinking skills 128
    Being truthful and straightforward 130
    Putting your client's interests before yours 131
Chapter 22 Participating in Professional Organizations 133

Part 5 Media Matters 137

Chapter 23 Out of One, Many 139
    Do the rights thing 141
    Who owns it? 141
Chapter 24 On Intellectual Property 143
    Copyright notices 143
    Citing the work of others 144
    Fair use 145
    Licensing fees 147
    Protecting your intellectual property 147
    A risk of writing 150
    Pure theft 150
    The funniest case 151

x GOING IT ALONE

Chapter 25 Twelve Tips for Becoming a Confident Presenter 153
Chapter 26 Some Presentation Tricks I Have Learned 161
    Open big 161
    Colorful flip charts 162
    Humor doesn't hurt 162
    Quiet questioners 163
    Let's get moving 163
    Door prizes 164
    Other random tips from the experts 164

Part 6 Writing Your Way to Success 167

Chapter 27 You Are What You Write 169
    Choosing a role model 170
    Focusing on clarity 171
    Acquiring the information 172
    Developing a style 173
Chapter 28 Four Eyes Are Better Than Two 175
    Take a look yourself 175
    Enlisting other eyes 176
    Copy editing 178
    Developmental editing 180
    Check it carefully 181
    Proofreading 182
    Using speech-recognition software 183
    When it's all your responsibility 184
Chapter 29 Writing for Magazines, Websites, and Blogs 185
    Knowing your audience 185
    Fitting in 186
    Delighting the editor 187
    Dangling the bait 187
    Setting the hook 188
    You have arrived! 189
Chapter 30 You Say You Want to Write a Book? 191
    Why write a book? 192
    How do you learn? 193
    Some book-writing recommendations 194
Chapter 31 Getting Your Book into Print 199
    Targeting a niche 200
    The elevator pitch 202
    Choosing a publisher 203
    The proposal 204
    The contract 207
    Making commitments 211
    Staying on track 212

Chapter 32 Being Your Own Publisher 215
    Self-publishing: Cheap 215
    Self-publishing: Less cheap 218
    Self-promotion 223

Chapter 33 On Co-Authoring a Book 225
    Requirements for requirements 226
    Across the miles 226
    Planning the collaboration 228
    Tracking status 228
    The result 230

Bibliography 233

Acknowledgments 235

About the Author 237

Index 239

Introduction

I have been self-employed as a software development and process improvement consultant since early 1998. I began doing this sort of work even earlier, while I was still working for a large corporation. This book is based on my Consulting Tips & Tricks blog, which I launched to share some of the insights I have accumulated over the years. I wish I had had a resource like this available when I was embarking on my consulting career.

Even if you don't work in information technology, you're sure to find a lot of information in this book that applies to being an independent consultant in other fields. And even if you aren't an independent consultant at the moment, you'll discover many useful tips about giving presentations, writing for publication, and working with others. My examples are drawn primarily from my personal experience in the software world. However, you can readily adapt the ideas and actions I suggest here to your own domain.

How I got here

By way of background, let me describe how I got started in the consulting business. After obtaining a PhD in organic chemistry from the University of Illinois, I began my professional career in 1979 as a research scientist at Kodak in Rochester, New York. Computer programming was my second interest after chemistry. For several reasons, I moved into software development at Kodak full-time in 1984. Six years later I took over as the manager of the small software group I was in.

I began learning as much as I could about software process improvement through books, periodicals, and conferences. Soon I found myself helping other groups inside Kodak with various aspects of software development, thus serving as an internal consultant. Ultimately I took a position leading software process improvement efforts in one of Kodak's digital imaging technology areas. Shortly before I left the company, I was guiding process improvements in Kodak's web development group, the people who bring you kodak.com.

In the early 1990s I began giving presentations at conferences, while I continued to write magazine articles about various aspects of software development and management. In 1994 I received my first invitation to speak at another company on some of the work I'd been writing about. More such opportunities quickly arose, thanks to my increasing visibility as a conference speaker and author. Soon I was providing consulting and training services for other companies on my vacation time, while I still worked full-time at Kodak. This was all done with my management's knowledge and approval. It was a safe way to ease into a consulting career.

My first book, *Creating a Software Engineering Culture*, was published in 1996 while I was still at Kodak. Shortly thereafter, a well-known software consultant and author asked me when I was going to leave the corporate world and hang out a shingle as an independent consultant. My initial reaction was that this seemed pretty risky, considering that I like to eat every day. But after reflection, I decided to give it a shot.

I officially launched my own one-person consulting company, Process Impact, in December of 1997. A few months later I left Kodak to see how things might go on my own. I figured I could always get a real job again if consulting didn't work out for whatever reason. As it happened, being an independent consultant, trainer, and author has worked out just fine for me.

Being self-employed

Some consultants find work through agencies. Others are employed full-time by a company that contracts their consulting services out to clients. However, with one brief exception very early on, I've always worked on my own through Process Impact. (Incidentally, I have found that, even in a one-person company, management is unreasonable and uninformed, and the staff are all lazy with bad attitudes.) When I started out, I knew little about this new mode of employment, yet I had few resources to learn from.

This book is based primarily on my personal experiences while being self-employed. Several other consultants also contributed chapters to share their experiences and perspectives. Many of these tips also apply to people—sometimes called consultants—who are engaged in staff-augmentation contracting relationships as temporary corporate employees. Some of our topics might not be as important to consultants who are employed by larger companies rather than being on their own.

I learned several things about consulting early on. First, I was fortunate to get much more work than I thought I might. That was a relief, as many new consultants struggle to stay afloat. Second, I discovered that I really enjoyed the flexibility of being self-employed. While at Kodak, I concluded that I do not need to be managed and I do not enjoy being a manager, so self-employment in a one-man shop has suited me well. And third, I found that there's a lot to learn about being a self-employed, self-managed consultant.

Casting a large net for knowledge

When I told my colleagues at Kodak I was going to leave and give consulting a shot, someone asked me how I'd be able to keep up with what was happening in the software industry if I didn't work on projects anymore.

That was an interesting question I hadn't considered. However, I quickly realized that, as a consultant, I could see how many projects and organizations operated, instead of just observing a few projects in one company for a prolonged period. I didn't have to make every mistake and climb every learning curve myself. Everyone I encountered at a client site, conference, or professional society meeting was a potential source of knowledge.

Gaining access to a wide variety of companies was far more educational than working inside a single microcosm with people steeped in the same corporate culture. It let me collect a breadth of information so I could recognize patterns of both effective practices and common problems. Then I could share that accumulated knowledge with others, for a very reasonable price. I'm pretty good at synthesizing knowledge from multiple sources, packaging it, and delivering it to others in a practical way. That's the essence of being a consultant.

There was another unobvious aspect regarding the knowledge you can—and cannot—acquire through consulting. I've done a lot of work in the field of software requirements over the years. People occasionally ask me, "Karl, what do the companies that are really good at requirements do?"

My reply is, "I don't know; they don't call me." That is, my clients are always people who know they want to improve how their teams perform certain aspects of their work. They invite me in to help assess those opportunities, provide knowledge through training or coaching, and assist them in migrating toward better ways of working. Companies that are already confident in their requirements engineering capabilities don't ask me to work with them. Hence, I have no way to learn what's working well for them unless they publish their experiences for all to see.

The other people who never call me are the ones who either aren't even aware that they have problems with requirements or don't opt to address them. That insight taught me that it's hard to sell a better mousetrap to people who don't realize they have mice.

How the book is organized

This book contains thirty-three chapters grouped into six parts. Part 1, "Setting up Shop," addresses laying the foundation for your consulting business, including letting the world know you're available and open for business, several different modes of consulting engagements, and the impacts that being a self-employed consultant can have on your life and your family.

Part 2, "On the Job," covers many realities I had to learn through trial and error; the errors weren't that much fun. Chapters address using checklists to keep all the activities you're juggling under control, techniques for engaging with clients in various situations, my concept of the ideal client, and some warnings about clients who can cause headaches for you and how to deal with them.

In Part 3, "Practicalities," you'll find valuable tips for such essentials as setting rates, managing your finances, and negotiating and crafting written agreements with your clients. Other chapters address establishing business policies and the important topic of purchasing appropriate insurance coverages.

Your business will probably start out a bit slow, leading you to look for ways to grow it. Part 4, "Building the Business," provides suggestions about how to do this. I describe how I established multiple revenue streams, so I could hear the "ka-ching" of incoming cash even when I wasn't doing anything related to the company. Other chapters in this section offer suggestions for landing both new and repeat business, along with some comments on participating in professional organizations.

Although I've always called myself a consultant, most of my independent work has involved delivering training. Teaching classes and making presentations are common consultant activities, so Part 5, "Media Matters," offers many tips for delivering effective presentations with confidence. It also describes ways to leverage your intellectual property repeatedly through different media formats, as well as addressing some important issues of copyright, fair use, and managing your valuable intellectual property.

Written communication is a core skill for any consultant. Hence, the book closes with Part 6, "Writing Your Way to Success." Publishing is a way to simultaneously share your knowledge with the world and market your expertise. This final set of chapters provides a wealth of information about writing for publication, including magazines, websites, blogs, and books. A prolific author once said that you can't consider yourself a good writer until you've written at least one hundred thousand words. My books alone total just over one million words. It's not for me to say if I'm a *good* writer, but I've learned a few useful things along the way, which I share in Part 6.

A supplemental web page to accompany this book is provided at https://tinyurl.com/goingitalone. It lists several other books on consulting that I've found helpful. It also provides links to numerous useful items described in these pages, including sample templates for client agreements, book proposals, checklists for your consulting activities, and a list of collaboration tools for remote consulting.

Some caveats

Let me emphasize that nothing in this book should be construed as legal advice. I am neither an attorney nor an accountant. You should consult with appropriate professionals if you have questions regarding legal matters, including finances, taxes, insurance, contracting, and how to structure your company.

Also, you might conclude that certain approaches I've found to be valuable are a poor fit for your situation. In that case, it would be silly to take my advice. Instead, look for the idea behind each recommendation here and see if there is some thoughtful way to adapt that to your situation. As with all such writings, your mileage may vary from mine.

Why to keep reading

I wish I had had a mentor to rely on for assistance, to answer the countless questions I had when starting out as an independent consultant. There's so much I needed to learn, from essential matters like how to find clients and how much to charge, down to minor practicalities such as how to uniquely identify invoices. (I use a code with an abbreviation for the client's name, the current year, and a sequence number within the year, such as IC1704 for the fourth invoice I submitted to client InfoCorp in 2017.)

Perhaps this book can serve as a useful resource for you if you're pursuing a career path similar to the one I chose. Even if you're not aiming to be an independent consultant, I'm confident you'll find plenty of information here that will enhance your own professional capabilities.

Part 1

Setting Up Shop

Chapter 1

Hanging Out the Shingle

I've known several knowledgeable and talented people who declared themselves to be consultants but never got enough work to make a living at it. The message I got from these experiences was that

> **It doesn't matter how good you are if nobody knows you're there.**

One man's experience particularly sticks in my mind. I'll call him Kevin here.

Kevin was very bright and had considerable experience in the broad domain of software process improvement. One day he decided to leave his corporate job to become a consultant. However, Kevin made some mistakes getting started.

To begin, he didn't take the necessary actions to let prospective clients know that he was available and could be helpful to them. Kevin never selected an official company name and never developed a website to market his services. He published very few articles in software magazines or on websites. These are good ways to establish some name recognition. Blogging is another useful technique, as is being an active contributor to blogs and discussion forums, such as those on LinkedIn. If people realize you have good ideas and useful information to share, they might want to learn more about you and possibly hire you.

Kevin did give several presentations at software conferences. Unfortunately, he didn't understand that the types of presentations and tutorials that one typically delivers at conferences might not have a good market in the corporate world. Even if you do get invited into a company to give a short talk it won't pay much, and there's only a small chance that it will lead to longer engagements.

Kevin also positioned himself in too narrow a specialty, just a couple of software engineering subdomains. In my experience, few organizations bring in consultants to help in those particular areas, important though they are. You're better off targeting the large market, not a small niche.

The net result of all this was that Kevin never gained much traction as an independent consultant. Eventually, he had to go back into corporate employment to have a reliable income.

You can learn from Kevin's experiences as you chart your own path for independent consulting in any field. Somehow, I was very fortunate. I always had all of the work I wanted to do when I was an active consultant. Maybe I just hit the sweet spot in terms of developing expertise, training materials, and other resources in areas that were in demand, such as requirements engineering and software quality. But I think I did take some of the right actions too.

Choose a good name

I thought long and hard about what to name my company. Some consultants don't use a company name at all, just their own name: "J. Fred McGillicutty, Independent Consultant." It was important to me to look like a real company though. I didn't want to call myself something like the Wiegers Consulting Group or Wiegers & Associates. You might be surprised at how many such-named companies have but a single employee—no group, no associates.

After considerable contemplation, I realized that my business goal was to have an impact on the processes that software organizations use to build their products, and for those processes to have an impact on the organization's business success. Hence the name I chose for my one-person company: Process Impact.

Incidentally, Process Impact does have a company slogan: "Our employee is our greatest asset." And we really believe that.

There are various ways you can set up a consulting company, ranging from sole proprietor, to limited liability company, to S corporation. In Chapter 14, "Money Matters for the New Consultant," Gary K. Evans describes these various options.

I have always been a sole proprietor, just me with no employees. I registered my business name in each state in which I lived as a sole proprietorship, which is officially "Karl Wiegers dba Process Impact." DBA means "doing business as," although in the state of Oregon where I now live it's also referred to as "doing business under an assumed name." That sounds a bit shady, but it's just the phrasing the state uses.

As a sole proprietor I can set up a bank account or credit card in the name of the business. I file Schedule C with my personal federal and state income tax returns each year to report my business income and expenses. I don't need to file any special tax forms besides that. I also had the Internal Revenue Service issue Process Impact an employer identification number (EIN). I give that number to my clients when they request a W-9 form for tax purposes, so I do not have to distribute my personal Social Security number all over the planet. Every bit of protection against identity theft helps.

Go online

When I launched the company I created a website immediately, ProcessImpact.com. I confess that this site is a bit dated and simple in design, but it offers a lot of useful content. I've always favored substance over glitz, function over form. I now have several other websites, including my personal site, KarlWiegers.com. I also created individual sites for each of my nontechnical books, like my novel, *The Reconstruction* (http://TheReconstructionBook.com). Even automobile repair shops have websites today. If you don't, will prospective clients think you are up-to-date on what matters to them?

Draw a crowd

Building a website is a good starting point, but you still need to attract people to that site. As time went by I posted increasing quantities of material there, including articles I had written, document templates and other useful work aids, and so forth. This kind of "bait" clearly draws visitors. The most popular item on my website, my software requirements specification template, has been downloaded many thousands of times. It's gratifying to create materials that others find useful. When people know your website offers valuable resources, they will set up links to it and come back for more later on, giving you more opportunities to sell them something at the right time.

Share what you know

Beginning way back in 1984, I wrote the first of more than 160 articles for numerous software magazines on a wide range of subjects: software engineering, requirements, project management, people management, quality, metrics, and process improvement. Early in my career I published up to ten articles per year with an average length of about three thousand words. Publishing generates good visibility and establishes the author's credentials in one or more areas of expertise. See Part 6 of this book, "Writing Your Way to Success," for many tips on writing for publication.

I began writing books even before I launched Process Impact. As of now, I have published seven books on software development and management, in addition to a memoir of life lessons titled *Pearls from Sand: How Small Encounters Lead to Powerful Lessons* and a novel, *The Reconstruction*. Having your name on a book gives you both visibility and credibility. The research I did while writing each book also greatly broadened my knowledge. This is not to say that I am the world's expert on any particular topic. You only have to know a little more than the next guy to be helpful though.

Get on stage

Early in my career I spoke at as many as six or eight conferences per year, often delivering multiple presentations at each event. This is a way to directly reach hundreds of people a year with your message. You know your career is progressing when conference producers invite you to submit papers, to sit on panels, and ultimately to deliver keynote presentations. As you gain recognition, you can get paid increasing amounts for your presentations. The conference fee is virtually always waived for speakers.

I've also presented many talks at meetings of professional organizations throughout the country. If you can find such organizations close to home, that raises your profile in your own community and presents the opportunity for generating local work. Any work that does not involve taking an airplane is fine with me. Over the years, I've developed more than two dozen short presentations on a wide variety of topics. Local organizations are good places to try out and polish a new presentation before you take your show on the road.

It all adds up

Doubtless it was the combination of all these activities that helped the software world become aware of my presence and capabilities. As a result, I was fortunate to make a decent living as a consultant and trainer. I never had to think about going back to work in a larger company. At this point, I don't think I could.

If you believe you have something valuable to offer, think about various ways you can let the world—or at least the part of the world that might give you money—learn of your existence and talents. It just might pay off.

Chapter 2

Hey, World, Here I Am!

Contributed by Gary K. Evans

> *Gary K. Evans is an independent agile consultant. He has spent two decades helping Fortune 500 companies incorporate agile methods and object-oriented techniques. He is a Certified Scrum Master, an Agile Coach, and a SAFe 4 Program Consultant.*

So you've decided to leave the corporate world and start out on your own. Congratulations! It's a big step. It can be kind of scary, leaving the comfortable security of a corporate womb with its reliable salary, decent benefits, advancement opportunities, and network of co-workers. Not everyone has the self-discipline to treat their home as their workplace. If you have small children you will have special adjustments to make so home life continues smoothly. The abrupt shift to working in isolation can be jarring if you've always been used to having a lot of people around for both professional and social interactions. Before you make the leap, think carefully about how you might react to those sorts of changes.

When you're an independent, you have full responsibility for everything that happens in the company. Those who take best to self-employment are the self-starters who can chart their own career paths and work independently. Being able to work alone and to switch easily between work contexts is a definite advantage.

You'll need to find your own employment opportunities, which means showing initiative, patience, and creativity in how you present yourself to potential clients. In addition to your own professional skills, you'll have to become a little bit of a marketer, accountant, writer, presentation designer, and office administrator. Whether you're out of jobs, coffee, or notepads, it's your problem. So let's see how you might start lining up those all-important clients to get the ball rolling.

Marketing you!

Finding work isn't the same as waiting for work to find you. A business plan of "Make lots of money" isn't a plan—it's a wish, not unlike "Win the lottery and retire." To become a successful consultant, you must have a plan. Think hard about what you do best, and build on your strengths. If you're uncomfortable around strangers or can't articulate in fifteen seconds the value you will bring to the client, attempting to go it alone may be rather unrealistic for you. If you're not interested in marketing, bookkeeping, or the many other nontechnical tasks required to run even a one-person business, plan on hiring—that means paying—someone to do these for you.

To find work, you must actively seek it out. This means marketing yourself. But don't limit yourself always to the same channels; your options will change over time.

When I started out, my first client fell right into my lap. I had invested fifteen years working for a well-known computer company until I, along with one-third of the other employees in my facility, received my severance notice. I hit the ground running, looking for a full-time job, but I was overqualified for every position I interviewed for. Then a New York company heard about the layoff and contacted me because I had the skills they needed.

For my next three or four engagements, I found work primarily through third-party groups who marketed me. On every engagement, I met people and cultivated relationships. In a short time, those relationships became a marketing channel as I began obtaining work from word-of-mouth recommendations. By expanding my base from just programming and design to teaching object-oriented technology, I aligned myself with several large object-oriented (OO) software companies. When consulting positions were sparse, my training work served as a safety net. And, after teaching various OO courses (of varying quality) marketed by these companies, my dissatisfaction with them led me to start writing and marketing my own training courses.

Next, I attempted cold-call marketing, with limited success. At the end of 1998, I made a conscious decision to try a more aggressive marketing plan, so I created a website. Then I started speaking at professional conferences. In 1999, I began writing magazine articles on object technology and object-oriented software development and modeling tools. I soon had the privilege of being asked to serve as a judge for the prestigious Jolt Awards for software productivity, a position I held for eleven years. And a few years ago I started a second business to produce a commercial software product for people who want to manage their nutrition and health.

My point is this: you must continually step out of your comfort zone. I'm not really kidding when I say that I'm now comfortable only when I'm out of my comfort zone.

Dealing with third-party placement

If you're an independent consultant, this doesn't mean you'll always have to find your own clients. Especially in the beginning of your independent career, you might find ready-made opportunities through third-party placement or system integration groups. Some of my best work experiences have come in this way. They handle the marketing, cold calls, payroll, and other details; I do the technology. The only downside is that they get paid from my pay.

Don't fall into the trap of whining about this, however. Recognize that the third party you're working through has to make money too. After all, they are doing the marketing, bookkeeping, and so on. Should you care what margin they are making from you?

My position is simple: I have no right to know the margin, and I don't care what it is. If I decide to work at $45 or $75 per hour and discover that the placement group is charging $125 per hour for me, so what? If $45 or $75 per hour meets my goals, I'm satisfied.

Grousing over someone else's margin is bad public relations, earning you the label of malcontent. Then you won't get any more work through that group.

Negotiate, never demand. Keep your eyes and ears open, and if you learn what the third party is charging for you, just sit on that information until the next contract renewal or project. Concentrate on what you must do to make yourself worth $100 per hour, and let the placement group worry about how to pass the increase on to the client. That's what they're getting paid to do. As you gain industry visibility and credibility, you might find that more prospective clients begin to contact you directly about providing services to them. When this happens, you'll rely less on third-party companies and contractors to locate work for you.

Independent consulting is a way of working that has become common in many industries. It seems destined to increase as our economy continues to mutate into integrated, electronic cottage-industry services. It has tremendous reward potential, along with its downsides. You can slice and dice your independence almost any way you wish, but you must also take care of business. If you really think you want to be independent, carefully count the costs, get prepared, and charge ahead. It could well change your life forever.

Chapter 3

Modes of Consulting: What's Your Preference?

In his classic book *Flawless Consulting*, Peter Block described three types of roles that consultants might take on: expert, pair-of-hands, and collaborator. Each of these represents a different kind of interaction when working with clients and a different source of satisfaction for the consultant. In this chapter I will describe some of my experiences with these three modes of consulting engagements.

Outside looking in

As an expert, you're working with a client who has a problem and wants you to fix it. I'm working in the expert role when a client brings me in to deliver some training, perform a process assessment, or review some project deliverables or process documentation.

More than one client has told me, "You're here because the pain has become too great." The organization was suffering from problems resulting from ineffective practices and processes in some domain, and they hired me to help them rectify those problems.

Unfortunately, I cannot actually fix the problems in their organization. I can evaluate the current reality, identify areas ripe for improvement, and suggest root causes that lead to the pain. I can provide the clients with knowledge and resources that can help, and I can propose a roadmap for applying that knowledge on their projects. But it's up to the managers and the practitioners in the client organization itself to implement those actions effectively.

Many improvement actions also require culture changes. Those take time and must be driven from within.

I've found that when I perform a process assessment, whether formal and structured with a written report or simply by providing feedback based on informal discussions, I rarely tell clients things they don't already know. For the most part, my clients are aware of their pain points. However, they might not be able to get senior management to take the matter seriously or to provide the necessary resources to address the issues.

It's not unusual to have a manager who brings me in say, "Please tell these other people what I've been trying unsuccessfully to tell them for six months. They'll listen to you." For reasons I've never understood, it seems to be more acceptable to have an outside expert make the same observations and proposals that some in-house employees already have made. It helps that the consultant is independent of the local organizational politics and isn't caught up in the history of "the way we've always done things around here." The outside expert has the perspective of having worked with numerous other organizations and noted patterns of both effective and ineffective practices in the industry.

Some of the most fun I've had in the expert consulting mode involved sitting in a room at a client site for a day while a procession of people came in to discuss various random problems they were facing. I never knew what kind of question was going to come up next. It might be about getting customers engaged in requirements discussions, dealing with configuration management issues, or generating better estimates for project planning. I found these all-too-infrequent types of engagements stimulating and challenging. I really had to think on my feet to understand the situation quickly and try to come up with suggestions that were likely to be effective.

I've done a great deal of consulting that involved reviewing process or project deliverables—most commonly requirements documents—to point out errors and provide improvement recommendations. I'm functioning as an outside expert in this sort of engagement too. After having reviewed many sets of requirements over the years, I have an idea of what constitutes a good one and common problems to look for. This body of experience allows me to examine a client's requirements spec efficiently and spot many improvement opportunities. Of course, I can't confirm that the document contains the *correct* requirements for the project because I wasn't involved with defining the needs, interviewing customers, or otherwise eliciting requirements. But I'm very good at finding other kinds of problems that someone with less experience in writing requirements might overlook.

One more way in which you might work in the expert consulting mode is as an expert witness in a lawsuit. I had this experience just once. The project involved the vendor of a packaged software solution and a customer organization that had purchased the package and hired the vendor to perform some customizations and data migrations. One of the parties in the lawsuit hired me to determine the factors that contributed to the project's abysmal failure.

After studying numerous project documents, I concluded that the party whose attorney had hired me caused most of the problems. The attorney read my report, said thank you, paid me, and that was the end of that. I heard much later that the parties had reached a settlement, so I never had to testify. This engagement led to an article titled "See You in Court," in which I shared some advice about making such outsourcing projects more successful. Some consultants make a very good living working as expert witnesses, applying what they've learned from years of industry experience.

The idea man

When I'm working as an expert consultant I view my key responsibility as providing ideas, ideas that will help a client solve a problem or build software faster and better. Some solution ideas are better than others, so I try to generate a lot of them. For every ten ideas I come up with, I figure that about two will be ridiculous, two more might not be very effective or won't suit the culture, three others will be obvious, two of the remainder will be clever and novel to the client, and the final one will be brilliant. I need to produce enough ideas to get a nice handful of solid hits in those last two categories.

I use a mental test as a reality check on any advice I propose in consulting discussions or when I write a formal recommendation report. First, I consider whether the actions I'm suggesting have a high probability of actually solving the client's problem. That is, my proposal must be effective. And second, I ask myself if the client actually *could* implement my suggestions if he chooses to do so.

That is, what I'm proposing must be both pragmatic and appropriate for the client's culture and situation. Each practice that I have in mind must pass both of these checks before I deliver it to the client. The last thing I want to do is give clients advice that wouldn't help them, isn't realistically feasible in their world, or might do them more harm than good.

Roadblocks

Perhaps the biggest sources of resistance to input from an outside expert are NIH and NAH syndromes.

NIH means "not invented here." The solution proposed by an outside expert can be rejected because the affected practitioners didn't create the solution themselves, so they don't necessarily buy into it or trust it.

NAH means "not applicable here." I've often heard the claim "we're different" from clients who weren't interested in trying my recommendations. They thought that whatever I was suggesting might work in other places but certainly not in their environment.

Organizations and cultures do come in a variety of flavors, but there are also many similarities between them. For example, I think nearly all software-developing organizations can follow basically the same change control process. Citing NIH or NAH as a reason not to accept the consultant's recommendations is often a sign of resistance against change in general. If you detect either NIH or NAH symptoms, your challenge shifts from proposing solutions to considering how best to have those solutions fall on receptive ears.

And then what happened?

One of the frustrating aspects of working with a client as an expert consultant or a trainer is that I rarely learn what happens after I leave the client site. Unless the client has engaged me for some ongoing work, it's totally up to the organization to decide how to apply the training or recommendations I presented. Of course, I hope they will maximize their return on the investment they made in the engagement. But if they just keep on doing whatever it was they did before I came along, they'll get an ROI of zero. There's no way to find out what happened afterward unless the client opts to share that information with me.

Occasionally, I have received feedback about the outcome some time after I taught a class. Once I had a student in a public seminar who had taken a requirements class from me about a year earlier. He said that his company now had product champions serving as key user representatives for all of their projects, a practice I strongly advocate. He said this approach was really helping their projects be more successful.

Such anecdotes help validate that I am presenting ideas and practices that are practical and can lead to better results in organizations that learn how to make them work. Because my goal is to help organizations do a better job with my help than they could otherwise, it's always great to hear that someone has found my advice to be valuable.

Many hands make light work

When working in the pair-of-hands consulting mode, the consultant is providing a service that the client might be able to perform himself but for which the client lacks sufficient staff or time. The client defines the need and sets the project boundaries and expectations. The consultant then goes off and performs the work largely on his own, with the contact at the client site assessing the deliverables to ensure they are satisfactory.

Some companies, for instance, hire an experienced business analyst on a contract basis for a specific software development project. The consultant comes into the organization and performs the traditional BA tasks of identifying users, eliciting requirements, writing specifications, and so forth. Such short-term staff augmentation for a specific project is a pair-of-hands mode.

I have done a great deal of work for one client I'll call Jack over more than fifteen years. Jack leads the software center of excellence in a large product-development company. Much of my work for Jack has been off-site (that is, in my own home) consulting work in either the pair-of-hands or collaborative mode. Most of the pair-of-hands work has involved developing process descriptions, templates, and other work aids. Jack is sufficiently knowledgeable and experienced to do this kind of work himself, but he simply doesn't have the time or the skilled internal staff available to do it in a timely fashion. Therefore, he outsources the activity to me.

Jack carefully reviews each deliverable I create and we iterate, working back and forth, until he finds the final product acceptable. For the most part, though, Jack simply delegates the work to me. He relies on my domain knowledge and our previous agreement on the form and structure for such documents to feel confident that he'll get a product that makes him happy.

Frankly, I haven't always been totally comfortable producing process-related deliverables in this pair-of-hands fashion. I trust my experience and my ability to prepare sensible process documents, so that's not the issue. Rather, I am sometimes concerned about how readily the people in the client organization will accept process materials—or any other artifacts—created by an outside third party (remember NIH and NAH?).

I saw evidence of this issue when I worked at Kodak years ago. Certain departments would hire consulting companies to create templates or other process documents for them, but some practitioners would resist using those items. The artifacts were created by people who didn't know the organization well. Sometimes they weren't a great fit for what the client teams needed or expected, often being more elaborate than necessary.

I've worried about encountering this reaction when performing similar work for Jack. It hasn't turned out to be much of a problem in practice, partly because of Jack's credibility and reputation in the company and partly because of mine. Nonetheless, I believe that process-related deliverables are best created in a collaborative mode between a highly experienced consultant and members of the client organization. This helps the client staff buy into the new artifacts.

My consulting agreements with Jack always include a general description of the type of services I will be performing and a list of deliverables. Such an agreement is called a statement of work, or SOW. Most of the time this works fine. We generally have a good mind meld and need very little planning or scoping documentation. I understand what Jack is asking for, and I can accomplish the objective independently without demanding a lot of his time.

Sometimes, though, Jack asks me to do something novel. Neither of us has a clear idea at the outset of exactly what the desired outcome is. In those cases, I ask him to write a short vision statement using the following keyword template, which is described in Chapter 5 of my book *Software Requirements*:

For	[target customer]
Who	[statement of the need or opportunity]
The	[deliverable name]
Is a	[type of deliverable]
That	[major capabilities or key benefits]
Unlike	[current reality or process]
This Deliverable	[primary differentiation and advantages of new deliverable]

Jack usually grumbles a bit about having to write this vision statement because I'm asking him to think carefully about just what he wants out of the project. That's hard! But then he works through the keyword template and always comes up with a clear, one-paragraph, structured statement that keeps us wonderfully focused on our mutual objective. I highly recommend asking your client to write such a vision statement anytime the nature or goals of the consulting engagement are too fuzzy at the outset.

Teamwork

In the third type of consulting engagement, the collaborative mode, the outside consultant joins forces with members of the client organization to work on the project or solve the problem together. In contrast to the more independent work that characterizes the pair-of-hands mode, the collaborative mode involves frequent interactions between consultant and client to identify solutions, set priorities, make decisions, and create deliverables jointly. As an analogy, you could think of co-authoring a book as being a collaborative engagement, whereas hiring a ghostwriter to craft your memoirs would be a pair-of-hands type of engagement.

A client recently hired me for an extended off-site collaborative engagement. This financial services company wished to implement peer reviews as part of its architectural governance process. A manager at the company was familiar with my book *Peer Reviews in Software*, so he engaged me to help. The clients relied on my extensive experience to advise them on how to make peer reviews effective in their environment for a specific set of work products and review objectives.

One member of the client's staff worked closely with me on this project to define the review process. We then developed several hours of e-learning presentations to train their staff in the new approach. The client drafted the slides and key talking points for the presentations. Next, I fleshed out a script for each slide with a more detailed narrative. I have considerable experience giving presentations and developing e-learning training, so I could improve his initial slides for a more effective presentation. I also recorded the audio from the scripts and generated the e-learning presentations, since I was already set up to do all that.

This was a fine example of collaboration, with a consultant and a client employee working side-by-side (albeit remotely in this instance) to generate effective work products that were better than either participant could have created alone. It was also educational and enjoyable for both of us.

I enjoy the collaborative type of activities the most. It's fun to work with smart, creative, and energetic people. One thing I felt lacking in my career as soon as I became an independent consultant was the opportunity to kick ideas around with other people, scribble on a whiteboard together, get their feedback on work I've done, and put our heads together to come up with better solutions. I felt isolated. That's probably why I enjoy the collaborative engagements; they help fill that gap in my professional interactions.

The collaborative engagements are good learning opportunities as well. They always leave me better prepared for the next project, with a broader base of knowledge and experience to rely on when I confront the next thorny challenge.

I recommend that you keep these different consulting modes in mind when future client engagement opportunities arise. Understanding your own preferences will help you select those gigs that are likely to be most enjoyable and fulfilling. It's also a good idea to match the consulting mode with the needs of a specific project. Your client might ask to hire you to perform some work in a pair-of-hands mode, but your assessment of the project might indicate that a collaborative engagement would be more effective. Shaping the engagement's parameters to yield the best outcome is part of your responsibility as a consultant.

Chapter 4

The Consulting Lifestyle

Contributed by Gary K. Evans

> *Gary K. Evans is an independent agile consultant. He has spent two decades helping Fortune 500 companies incorporate agile methods and object-oriented techniques. He is a Certified Scrum Master, an Agile Coach, and a SAFe 4 Program Consultant.*

Anyone who's flirting with "going independent" must consider a number of issues. Contracting isn't just regular employment without a boss—it's *qualitatively* different from a traditional corporate position, and it's not for everyone. It affects both you and your family in a myriad of ways. It's not a move to undertake without carefully considering the implications.

Why be a consultant?

When I considered going out on my own, the fundamental question I had to face was: why do this? What inspires someone to walk away from the security of a salaried job?

The answer varies with the individual. Some want more income or more control over their professional lives. Others are running from a bad corporate position or seeking a challenging, exhausting world of untapped potential. Still others are forced into the choice by a layoff. Regardless, you should examine your motives ruthlessly.

Survey the field in which you wish to market your services and ask yourself if it can supply your financial needs on a sustained basis. In 1999, the Y2K problem put COBOL and RPG programmers in high demand, and many with those skills jumped to contract or independent work. But by the end of 2001, it was the end of the road for many who had only those skills to bring to the market. You can't let your skills go stale.

Be brutal in your self-examination. Remember, you never "work whenever you want to"—you work when work is around, because it might not be available when you want it. If the thought of cold calling gives you chills, perhaps you're not ready to take the plunge. Are you ready to always be looking for work? Are you ready to accept each holiday and vacation period as unpaid days? Give the potential downside serious consideration.

If you do decide to give consulting a fling, please do not burn your former employee relationships. You might despise the company you're leaving, but don't ever say so publicly, and that includes your social media accounts. You might think your former managers are all idiots, but if you ever speak of them publicly, make sure you describe only what they did right. You can never know if you might someday need to rely on those very people to hire you or to act as a reference. In 1993, I was part of a layoff by NCR Corporation in the United States. Five weeks later my first client was NCR-Canada, with whom I had had zero prior contact. You just never know what the future may bring. Keep it professional, never personal.

What if you move to consulting and then realize this really is not for you? Always have a backup plan, as well as some money in the bank. As I discuss below, consulting affects everyone in a family or relationship. You might find that the stress of job search, continual job uncertainty, weeks away from home, living in hotels, and eating meals alone is too high a price to pay. It all takes a toll. Eventually you might conclude that being an independent consultant is not a good fit, at least not now.

A simple recommendation if you want to test the waters of consulting is to plan to spend six to twelve months building a consulting presence, while retaining your full-time job. If you find yourself unemployed and the job market is good, you might be able to fill your calendar with consulting work and perhaps even capture some full-time offers as well. In the latter scenario, one approach I embraced was to offer my services to the potential employer on a contract basis for, say, three months, so we could "test drive" each other. This way I was building my consulting credentials and history. They had already acknowledged that they thought I would make a valuable addition to their full-time staff, so their risk was low.

Two of the facets I love most about consulting are the flexibility it offers and the creativity it allows. You just have to think of how you can construct a win-win both for your own goals and for the company engaging you. If you decide that independent consulting is not to your taste or the work just doesn't materialize, consider joining a small consulting firm that needs your skills or even returning to a full-time employment position.

The notion that consulting isn't a job, but rather is a way of doing a job, came home to me when I read Alan Weiss's excellent book *Million Dollar Consulting*. Essentially, we must have a field in which to conduct our consulting. You can choose to align yourself with a product, a vendor, a technology domain, or a platform. But beyond those choices, you must also find a focus, which should become your personal mission statement. Without this, you'll never know when to say no to a job offer. And if you don't say no to the wrong engagement, you won't be available to say yes when the right one comes along.

It's a family business

Unless you're a hermit, don't fool yourself: consulting affects everyone in a family or a close relationship. For contractors as well as regular employees, time away from home takes its toll. In the expanding global marketplace, our industry requires more traveling than ever before. I recently looked at my frequent-flier balance with Delta Airlines. It's over five hundred thousand miles, even after cashing in several tens of thousands of miles for family flight tickets. And this is only for Delta, which I have flown just four times in the past three years! I estimate I logged very close to one million miles across all airlines in my first seventeen years of consulting.

But even the grinding tedium of air travel does not compare to the stress that comes at the end of a contract when no other opportunity is present. Essentially, you're out of a job—again and again. The stress of finding clients, negotiating fees, terms, and schedules, and delivering what you promise can be a killer if you don't have confidence in your abilities and support from those closest to you.

All of this will take a physical toll also. I have been very active all my adult life, lifting weights and playing soccer. This physical activity is crucial to maintaining both my mental and physical well-being. Make time for yourself so you can stay as healthy as possible and be strong enough to support your family even when you're not there with them. Having work is great, but you need to take enough breaks to stay mentally and physically healthy.

When you disappear into a distant town, don't become just a vague memory for your loved ones. When I travel, I call home every single night to talk with my wife and my children so I can still have a presence at home. When my children were small, I helped them with homework over the phone. Math isn't easy to do by voice alone. All those years ago my wife would fax or email the kids' assignment sheets to me, and I would go over the assignments with them, usually sending back examples of how to solve the problems.

It would have been infinitely better to be sitting at the kitchen table with them, but I could not, so this was a creative alternative. It required more effort from me, but it helped them and kept us in touch. And that's the whole point. Today's technology has made maintaining a family presence so much easier, but you are still away from home.

If you work out of a home office and you have small children, you will face a special challenge. When I started consulting, my children were seven and one. My seven-year-old understood the signal of my office door: when Daddy's door is closed, he is working and you should not interrupt him. He will come out later to play. But my one-year-old knew no such restraint. When he heard me through the door typing or talking on the telephone, all he knew was: Daddy's home. . . play time! It broke my heart—and his—for me to have to gently move him out of my office so I could work.

For several years I resorted to setting up shop with my laptop in a local public library several days a week. It was there in a (really) little room that I wrote my Object-Oriented Analysis and Design course of more than seven hundred pages. Getting out of the house insulated me from the many appealing distractions.

Another unanticipated possibility if you're working out of your home is that your spouse or partner really might not like having you hanging around all day. You think you are at work, but your partner sees you as interloping on what was private turf. "This is my kingdom during the day, when you should be at an office somewhere else!" is the unstated attitude. Your partner might not hesitate to ask you to fix the cord on the vacuum, invite you to drive to the hardware store to look at faucets, or generate any number of other innocent interruptions. Those interruptions do add up and sap your productivity. You could find yourself staring at a screen at 10:00 p.m., realizing you accomplished nothing billable that day on the project your client is paying you to complete.

Expect that your days will not go as smoothly as you hope, and accept that both you and your family will have to make some lifestyle changes and accommodations. Assess yourself and your loved ones honestly. If you do decide to take the plunge, put the burden on yourself, so it looks easy from your family's point of view.

Working with family members

Some people who set up a new self-employment business intend to work with some of their family members, either officially as paid employees or unofficially just to help out. In some cases this works out well. In others it can seriously threaten domestic tranquility.

One of my colleagues shared the following story: "When I started my consulting business I had a second phone line installed in the house for my home office. Occasionally I wouldn't be able to get to my phone in time when it rang, so I asked my wife if she could please answer it when that happens and take a message. She kind of glared at me. She had previously been a secretary for twenty-six years and had had enough of that gig. I explained that I was asking her to answer the phone not as my company secretary, but rather as the other person who lives in the house with me. That mollified her somewhat, but she still wasn't thrilled about it. Clearly, the consulting business was my company alone."

Before you decide to pull family members into your business, think carefully about the potential impacts on the family dynamics and economics. You might be passionate about your foray into the world of independent consulting, but your spouse, nephew, or second cousin once removed might not share your commitment to the cause. Sit down together to work out the specifics of expectations, communications, and compensation. A spouse who's already busy taking care of children and running the household while you're gallivanting around the countryside might not care to adopt any responsibilities for your business. She didn't have to help with your work when you went to a normal office; why should she now?

If a family member has the knowledge, time, and inclination to help out with certain aspects of your business, great. Bring him or her on board and treat it like a business relationship, but with someone you already know well and enjoy being around. Otherwise, either plan to do all the work yourself or hire an assistant when necessary to help out with small or periodic tasks.

Part 2

On the Job

Chapter 5

Make a List, Check It Twice

When I began giving presentations at software conferences in the early 1990s, most speakers used plastic transparencies on an overhead projector for their visuals. Only a handful of speakers had begun using laptop computers with Microsoft PowerPoint or other presentation software.

In those early days, I once presented a full-day tutorial at a local conference. I packed up my boxes of transparencies and headed to the conference site, clear across town from my home. Near the middle of my talk, I noticed that I was running out of plastic faster than I was running out of time. Suddenly I realized that I had brought only two of the four boxes of transparencies I needed for this full-day class. Uh-oh. Seriously embarrassing and unprofessional (a descriptor I strive mightily to avoid).

Fortunately, the man who was running the conference saved my bacon. I had sent him an electronic version of my presentation in advance, which he had installed on his laptop. After lunch I was able to complete my presentation using his laptop in lieu of my missing transparencies. That was my first live PowerPoint experience and among my most awkward professional mistakes.

That was a close call. I learned my lesson though. From then on I have *always* used a checklist to prepare for my speaking and consulting engagements. I already had created a travel checklist, but as this was a local event with no travel involved, I didn't bother to think carefully about what I needed to bring with me. I never made that mistake again.

My travel checklist has evolved over the years. I use it for both business and vacation travel. Different sections of the checklist remind me what to take along depending on which class I'm teaching. A separate section lists items to throw in the car when I'm driving somewhere instead of flying, like my favorite pillow and my stuffed teddy bear. (Just kidding about the teddy bear. Not kidding about the pillow.) I have a supplemental checklist for international travel that reminds me to pack my passport, visas, foreign currency, international driver's license, power plug adapters, and so forth.

I am religious about using the checklist to plan each trip and pack my bags. It helps me take along the right amount and the right kinds of clothing, all of my toiletries and medications, the right frequent-flier and car-rental cards, and the noise-canceling headphones that make long flights more bearable. It's also convenient to have a record of everything that's in my suitcase, should the airline's subterranean baggage-handling creatures devour it. Thanks to these checklists, I have never reached a destination and discovered that I was missing my laser pointer or a pair of socks.

You might scoff at my little checklists, but I tell you, they work. When I described my travel checklist to a fellow consultant, he chuckled, held up his index finger, and said, "My checklist has one thing on it: slides." But then he related the time he attended a conference to deliver a half-day tutorial, only to discover that he was scheduled to teach—but had not brought along materials for—a full day. It sounds like my colleague needs a better checklist.

You can see the current version of my travel checklist at https://tinyurl.com/goingitalone. That page also offers several checklists graciously provided by consultant Mike Cohn. One is a comprehensive travel packing list, which is nicely organized into clothes, Dopp kit (what I call a toilet kit), gadgets, and other categories. A second list provides a comprehensive reminder of all the items he needs for specific sorts of engagements. When you're teaching a class that involves a variety of student activities, you don't want to come up short on any of the necessary workbooks, cards, sticky notes, or other materials you need. My classes are simpler than some of Mike's, so I put all of that information right on my main travel checklist.

A third list from Mike is a planning form for a specific client engagement that provides a place to organize all the necessary information. It's easy to overlook some of these bits, to your peril. For instance, I always get the home and cell phone numbers for my primary contact at the client site in case I encounter travel difficulties on the way there. Mike's engagement checklist has a place to record that sort of useful information. I've needed those numbers a few times, like when an airline's pilots went on strike a couple of hours before I was supposed to fly from one client site to another in a different country. I simply couldn't get there; we had to reschedule the event.

Mike also shared some checklists that identify the things he must do to book a venue for a public class his company is presenting, as well as the items to take along when he's speaking at a professional organization. I suspect Mike's events all run smoother with the help of these planning aids.

Besides checklists, I've developed an assortment of other forms that I use for various purposes in my consulting and training business. They are nothing fancy, but if you need similar forms for your own business, you are welcome to download these from https://tinyurl.com/goingitalone and tweak them to suit your purposes. One is a form I use for tracking the time I spend doing offsite consulting at my home for a client. I provide these kinds of services on an hourly basis. I need to keep track of how much time I spend each month on project activities so I can send the client an appropriate invoice.

Perhaps this looks too lawyer-like to you. That's not the intent. I'm not trying to wring every dollar I can out of the client, but I do need an accurate record. I always round the time in the client's favor. If I ever have to do any rework because of a mistake I made, of course the client does not pay for that time.

I use the event tracking form on that download page to record information about events I have scheduled. There are many bits of information to keep track of, and there have been times in my career when I had numerous events pending or awaiting payment. I don't want to overlook anything associated with such activities. I use this form to note when I sent out my speaking agreement and when it was returned with a signature, as well as the dates I made my travel reservations for flights, hotel, and rental car. I can log the date I sent the course handout master to the client for duplication, and also when I ordered copies of my books to be shipped to the client for a class I'm teaching.

I don't want to arrive at a destination without my presentation files, so the form lets me note whether I have loaded all the necessary files onto my laptop (L) and also onto a backup flash drive (B). Finally, I record when I completed the event, when I submitted the invoice to the client, and when I received payment. Putting all of these items onto a single page shows me at a quick glance where each of my business events stands.

You might think my checklists are a waste of time, just another example of unnecessary process overhead. Perhaps you're right. Let's do an experiment. We'll both pack for the same trip. I'll use my travel checklist to help me. You just do whatever you normally do to pack. We'll see who runs out of underwear first.

Chapter 6

No Easy Answers

I've spent a lot of time helping organizations improve the way they develop and manage the requirements for software projects. Most people realize that this is a challenging task without many shortcuts. Yet some people have asked me questions in a way that suggests they hope I will give them a magic, easy solution to a difficult problem. If only I could.

For instance, someone once asked me during a training course, "What should you do if your requirements are written in Japanese?" This American organization was collaborating with a Japanese company, which supplied them with the initial requirements written in their native language. I could think of only four possible ways to deal with this situation:

- Learn to read Japanese
- Have someone translate the requirements they receive from Japanese into English
- Persuade the Japanese originators to write them in English in the first place
- Have a Japanese speaker work closely with the Japanese company to do the translation as the requirements are being developed

This seems obvious to me. But I could tell from the inquirer's expression and tone of voice that he was really hoping I knew of a painless solution to this problem. I'm pretty sure he already knew that there was none. (This was long before services like Google Translate existed.) Nevertheless, he asked. I hope he wasn't too disappointed by my response.

I would like nothing better than to offer amazingly effective and easy solutions to such challenges. Just think how much I could charge as a consultant if I knew those secrets! Alas, there are no such secrets. There are no magic wands, talking mirrors, genies in lamps, or all-knowing wizards. Sorry.

In a second case, a business analyst told me that another BA she worked with sometimes proceeded with his part of their project without respecting the needs and limitations that her portion of the work imposed on his. She wanted ideas about how to deal with this problem. My suggestion was to try to forge a more collaborative relationship with the other BA so they could identify their interdependencies, partition the work appropriately, and work together effectively. However, she was reluctant to talk to the other BA. She didn't seem to think the strategy I proposed was feasible in her environment, so she dismissed it out of hand.

I wonder if she thought I had a secret code phrase that would make this other analyst cooperate with her. Perhaps she was seeking some trick to make him more reasonable. The best I could do was to propose that she sit down with the other players on this kind of project and have everyone tell their peers, "Here's what I need from you for us jointly to be successful. What do you need from me?" All project participants should be able to have this conversation.

That's a more collaborative approach. It's not magic, it might be uncomfortable, and it might fail if the other participants refuse to play along. Sadly, not all project participants are interested in being flexible and collaborative. I point out at the beginning of all of my training classes that none of the practices I'm going to describe are likely to work if you're dealing with unreasonable people.

People sometimes appear to be unreasonable when they are merely uninformed. I have seen apparently unreasonable people change their tune when presented with information they were lacking. But if certain people you're trying to work with truly are being uncooperative, that's an interpersonal issue, not a technical problem.

This desire for painless solutions also shows up when planning a project. Project managers or team members often are asked to estimate how much time or money it will take to accomplish a proposed—but typically ill-defined—body of work. If you're asked for such an estimate, you might offer an answer your manager or your customer doesn't like. Perhaps it requires more resources than are available or it will take longer than the customers desire. These disappointed people can exert considerable pressure on you to change your estimate, even if there's no good reason to. Simply cutting the estimate doesn't make the project smaller or reduce how long it will take to do the work. It just moves everyone deeper into a fantasy world. It's comforting, perhaps, but it's not helpful.

I saw a striking example of this phenomenon once with a project manager I'll call Melanie. A senior manager asked Melanie in a heavily-attended company meeting how long it would take to complete a particular project. Melanie replied, "Two years." This manager said, "That's too long; I need it in six months." So how did Melanie respond? She simply said, "Okay." In other words, she just pretended it was feasible to execute this project in six months. I'm not a huge fan of pretending at work.

But what *really* changed during those few seconds? Nothing! The required work did not shrink by a factor of four. The productivity of Melanie's team did not instantly quadruple. No additional people were assigned to the project. Nor were Melanie's estimation method and assumptions questioned. Melanie simply said what she knew the senior manager wanted to hear.

Not surprisingly, the project took more than two years. Even thoughtful estimates often are optimistic and don't account for risks, unexpected events, and the inevitable scope growth.

It does no one any favors to pretend that the world is different from how it really is. It's fruitless to seek magic solutions for difficult problems when there aren't any. At times I'm not that crazy about reality, but it's all I have, so I have to deal with it. So do my clients, whether they like it or not. Sometimes, that means we encounter technical barriers or interpersonal challenges we cannot easily fix, no matter how badly we want to.

Instead of searching for secret solutions, we have to rely on skilled technical practitioners, adroit project managers, and leaders who can steer teams of people toward effective communication and collaboration. That's a special kind of magic in itself.

Chapter 7

Consultants as Legitimate Leaders: The Goldilocks Approach

Contributed by Jeanette Pigeon

Jeanette Pigeon, President and CEO at aBetterBA IT Solutions, Inc., is a certified business analyst professional who has worked in government, healthcare, higher education, and marketing industries and is a business analyst leadership subject matter expert. Contact her at abetterba@gmail.com.

Today, many people are protesting a perceived lack of legitimate leadership in private industry and government. By "legitimate leadership," I mean power that is exercised fairly and is based on a relationship of trust between a leader and followers. Followers grant this leadership of power and authority because they believe an individual exhibits the characteristics to lead and create win-win outcomes. A leader is a guide whose ideas define the paths for a group to follow to a shared goal or outcome in a collaborative way.

As a consultant, you may have wondered how you can effectively lead a team of professionals during the short tenure of your contract assignment. Because you are an outsider to the organization and have a limited amount of time to complete a project, you need to establish yourself quickly as a capable leader who can win over the hearts and minds of others. They need to see you as a confident and highly competent guide who knows the path for them to follow, reinforced through consistency of behavior and communication, and built upon a foundation of trust.

The big question is how to build this trust quickly. Do you try to satisfy everyone by being overly friendly and flexible? Or do you aggressively assert your dominance so everyone knows who's in charge? I recommend you use a Goldilocks approach: not too weak, yet not too strong

As in the Brothers Grimm's tale of "Goldilocks and the Three Bears," legitimate leadership is earned using a just-right approach. Being either too weak or too strong will not develop team cohesion or motivate others to pursue a common goal to reach successful outcomes. These approaches are one-sided; neither establishes a trusting relationship. To build trust, you must practice the "3 Cs" of legitimate leadership: Confidence, Competence, and Consistency of behavior and communication. Practicing the "3 Cs" will help you establish and maintain a relationship of mutual trust to create win-win outcomes.

Let's consider each of the three possible approaches and their efficacy in creating legitimate leadership.

Too weak

You attempt to build trust by trying to satisfy everyone. You're unable to articulate a common path. You appear to have no sense of direction, to be a flip-flopper with no consistent vision. When you speak, you are inarticulate or inconsistent about the team's goals or how they can achieve those goals. You try to be nice to your team members and give them as much time and leeway as they want, even though this might conflict with what your project actually requires to succeed. Your stakeholders don't see substantive progress, so their expectations are not met. As a result, you create a leadership vacuum.

In a leadership vacuum, one or more team members may rise up and become implicit leaders of the team, undermining your leadership authority. When working in a matrix organization or with a newly formed team, members don't collaborate effectively. Some might constantly challenge your authority over the team.

In the process of trying to accommodate everyone individually, you satisfy no one. You do not appear to be a competent leader of a fully-functioning team. Your confidence in the face of these obvious capability and trust gaps makes you appear out of touch and ineffective as a leader.

Too strong

You dominate the team members and other stakeholders and create a dictatorship. Team members are dragged down a path that is fraught with difficulty, delays, and failed projects. Stakeholders and team members become intimidated. They won't open up to you and tell you the truth. Instead of establishing a trusting relationship with your people, you achieve the opposite. You ignore the organizational culture and hierarchy, and you reject or fail to solicit input from others. People resent you and what you are trying to achieve. The results can include a failure to follow your lead and perhaps even attempts to sabotage your efforts.

Leading others through fear and intimidation is never effective when collaboration is your goal. Although you might appear to the stakeholders to be a competent subject matter expert, you don't appear effective as a leader, so you don't earn the trust or legitimate leadership of your team or your stakeholders.

Just right

You've taken the time to meet with key members of your team and other stakeholders. You've established a bond with each of them as a person and as a professional. You are sensitive to their needs and desires, and you have set appropriate expectations about working together and what will be achieved. You maintain an open door policy, encourage questions and ideas, and work openly to address concerns and to mitigate risks.

As issues arise, you seek to resolve them fairly and face-to-face without creating added tension or causing others to become defensive. You walk the talk and roll up your sleeves, working alongside the team members when necessary. Your team is cohesive; the team members understand how to engage you and what you expect of them. They are not afraid to seek your counsel and will let you know if issues arise before you're aware of them. Morale is high; people put in extra effort without being asked. Stakeholders are satisfied and they appreciate how efficiently and effectively your team performs.

Legitimate leadership is the reward of those who build a relationship of trust and exhibit the "3 Cs": confidence of leadership, competence as a subject matter expert, and consistency of behavior and communication. The just-right approach to legitimate leadership will allow you to more easily assert the leadership role among your team and stakeholders, enjoying the collaborative synergy that results. Your team and its stakeholders will enjoy working with you, satisfied in having achieved the stated goals. A series of such win-win outcomes will contribute to a long and professionally fulfilling consulting career.

Chapter 8

OMG, What Have I Done?! Anticipating Risks When Working with Others

Contributed by Vicki James

> *Vicki James is a certified Project Management Professional (PMP), a Certified Business Analysis Professional (CBAP), a certified PMI Professional in Business Analysis (PMI-PBA), and a Certified Scrum Master (CSM). Vicki has consulted with several Seattle-area companies. Most recently, she has found her ideal match as a permanent employee of Capital One and looks forward to a long career at the company.*

I quit my public-service project management job a few years ago to enter the world of independent consulting. I thrive on change and the idea of bringing new and better ideas, processes, and tools to as many people and organizations as possible. Only I made a mistake along the way. This mistake could occur with a variety of working relationships, including corporate employment, project collaborations, consulting for clients, and business partnerships.

The story begins about six weeks after I had left my civil service position, where I had been a business analyst and project manager for eleven years. I had started talking with one of the owners of a local technology company about subcontracting opportunities in both of those fields. Instead, they offered me a job as a salaried employee. Great! I could earn a salary doing what I wanted, consulting with different clients while helping the company expand its business opportunities. The difference was that my work would be through an established company rather than my own startup.

What did I have to lose? I was prepared to postpone establishing my own consulting business for one year as a worst-case scenario. This company hired me without even an interview, which seemed at the time like a vote of confidence and a sure sign of success. In hindsight, I went to work for them with too little information, and I paid the price.

Interviews are a funny thing. Most of us fear them. What questions will they ask? Will they like me? Will I sound knowledgeable? Do I have spinach in my teeth? I often counsel others who are considering a change that the interview is a chance for them to find out about the prospective employer and judge how well the company might align with the candidate's professional goals and expectations.

Too bad I did not listen to my own advice. I did not take the opportunity to explore how the company would help—or hinder—my own professional aspirations. Instead, I envisioned a world in which they would leverage my expertise to expand their own business, both in terms of client projects I took on and by relying on my experience and tendency to act to bring better process to my own work environment.

The management structure of the company consisted of four officers: three investors and a hired operations manager. By one officer's own admission, there was not a single decision maker. Instead, the company philosophy was management by consensus. This approach did not allow for serious consideration of my ideas for process improvement within the company.

I felt as if my expertise and experience were not valued because of this. Initially, I chalked it up to being the new girl on the block. Eventually, though, the reality became clear that adding another perspective to their dynamic would confuse things more than they already were in their leaderless decision-making processes.

Things began to unravel almost a year into the position, when they assigned me to manage a troubled project. I had been working directly with various clients on contract away from the central office and bosses until this time. It was when working with the bosses on managing a high-profile client that I began to recognize the extent of the differences in our business philosophies and professional ethics. Here are some examples of the struggles I encountered:

- Management often questioned and criticized my actions, decisions, and communications because we did not share the same client- and team-management principles. I am generally forthright and candid; I communicate everything to all. They preferred to hold information close to the vest. Rarely did a week go by that I was not "counseled" by one of the bosses. Often, this was after I previously had discussed some strategy with another boss. They did not have a shared philosophy among themselves, and I often paid the price for their lack of continuity.
- I am an analytical and process-oriented individual. In this fast-moving technology company, I always felt that projects were in chaos. The managers believed that process slowed down development and therefore billing; I don't agree.
- The management team as a whole did not buy into the value of project management. One or more bosses would often ignore or overturn my recommendations and actions in relation to project process, clients, and team development. On at least two occasions, the Chief Technology Officer made derogatory comments to me about "you project management types."

This was clearly a clash of working styles and values. I now realize that an interview and more exploration up front might have kept me from taking a job at a company where I would not be happy. I might have avoided the position altogether or been able to propose conditions of employment. Because I leapt at this appealing opportunity without performing due diligence, I missed an important opportunity to identify and manage some of the risks of working with other people. Instead, I spent fourteen months in a position that was not satisfying.

Different professional relationships come with different risks. I now see how important risk analysis is when I consider this from the perspective of an independent consultant and the opportunities that might come along. Let me give you some examples.

Clients

Some clients will come with a cost greater than the benefit you hope to receive. It may be that there is too little—or no—money if the client does not pay as agreed and you end up in the hole. There may be other financial consequences to the company, such as the cost of employee turnover or the impact on the company's reputation if things go badly.

Get to know your clients and document all agreements, both financial and operational, before beginning work. You always have the option to turn the work down. This should be given serious consideration when the risk is high.

Business partners

Taking on a business partner is much like getting married in the sense of financial and legal obligations. The unfortunate ending in either case is called "dissolution" and can be very damaging. You should understand your future business partner well to be able to identify the risks and benefits of working together. Risk mitigation is far easier and less painful than crisis resolution.

Collaborators

You will need to rely on your collaborators to uphold their end of the bargain and to treat you fairly when joining forces to complete a project. Get to know them. If you need to, check references either formally or informally. Discuss and document all agreements up front to avoid misunderstandings. I recently began collaborating with a colleague on a writing project. This time I was much more careful to consider what could go wrong and how likely it would be to happen. That's the essence of risk analysis.

Whether you're exploring a client–vendor relationship, an employee–employer relationship, or partnering with someone in a business or on a project, consider the following questions to begin recognizing the potential risks:

- Do you share a common vision for the business or project?
- Do you know, accept, and respect each other's work ethics, dedication, commitment, and constraints?
- Do your skills complement each other? For instance, do you have a skill your client lacks, or does one partner have a strategic, big-picture outlook for the company, while the other can focus on the details?
- Is there mutual respect for each other's expertise? That is, can you be confident that your ideas will be fairly considered, or does your client or partner believe she already has all the answers?

Once you've acquired more information, you can ponder further. What are the likely benefits of the collaboration? What can you imagine possibly going wrong? What impact could those outcomes have on you mentally, financially, or professionally? What is the likelihood of each of those risks materializing into an actual problem? Do the benefits outweigh the risks?

This is where I failed in my own situation. While I had considered the worst-case outcome of employment as deferring my move into independent consulting for a year, I did not take the time to adequately explore the range and likelihood of other potential unpleasant outcomes from taking this position. I hope you will gain some valuable insight from this experience so we can all learn from my mistake.

Chapter 9

The Dream Client

What makes an ideal client, a company or an individual you hope will call you back over and over? The best clients are fun to work with, appreciate your value, gain benefit from your contributions, and treat you well. They don't waste your time or make you feel as though you are wasting theirs. They pay you on time and without hassle. They present interesting challenges and opportunities that give you a chance to apply all of your skills and knowledge, as well as learning more.

I've been fortunate to have had several such clients over the years. My very first client, Sandy, was in that category, so I got a bit spoiled early in my consulting career. Sandy was a mid-level manager leading process improvement efforts in a company in Rochester, New York. I met her when I gave a presentation for a local professional group while I was still working at Kodak. She read my first book, *Creating a Software Engineering Culture*, and then she hired me to help with their improvement efforts in several capacities. I worked for Sandy and others in her parent company at various locations for several years.

Sandy and I worked together well and became good friends. We're still friends today. I like it when I stay friends with some of my clients long after our collaboration has ended. Some consultants prefer to maintain a professional distance from their clients. Not me. We can work together, exchange money for services rendered, and be friends without any of these various connections tangling each other up. It was great fun last spring when I just happened to bump into a former client, with whom I've stayed in touch for more than ten years, when we were both visiting a winery in Washington State. Totally random, and a real treat. Plus, the wine was excellent.

Sandy demonstrated another characteristic of a first-rate client. She was highly skilled at reading the politics of her corporate environment and navigating them successfully without getting caught up in the politics herself. She knew how to pitch proposed process changes in a way that would grab the right managers' attention and make the changes politically acceptable.

This ability made Sandy highly effective at incorporating the changes we advocated into her organization so they yielded the maximum benefits. It was informative to watch her chart the political and management minefields and cruise around the obstacles. If you can't read the politics and steer them to your advantage, then you might be victimized by them.

I've worked for another dream client, Bill, for some fifteen years. Bill leads the process improvement effort in a large company with dozens of divisions worldwide that make complex software and hardware products. I've provided many types of services to Bill's company, including teaching classes, presenting at their internal technology conferences, writing process documents, reviewing requirements specifications, and consulting on a variety of special projects. Bill employs several consultants who specialize in various areas to augment his personal efforts. He can direct opportunities to whoever is the best fit and is available when needed.

Bill is an ideal client for many reasons. He gives me as much work as I'm interested in doing, while respecting the times I decline an offer from him. He has never given me any hassle on contracting, always accepts my standard speaking and consulting agreements, never challenges my fees, and insulates me from his corporate legal department. Bill has referred me to managers of numerous divisions in his large company to provide training or consulting services. My dozens of invoices have always been paid on time.

Bill has also been generous about sharing ownership of our work products. Occasionally he has asked me to develop some artifact, such as a document template or a process description, that I was interested in adding to my own collection for use with other clients. Bill has always agreed to do so, in exchange for a discounted rate on my consulting fee for that part of the work.

On top of all that, Bill and I have become good friends. We've socialized outside our professional engagements, visited some wineries together, and even stayed at each other's homes, even though we live more than twenty-five hundred miles apart.

It has been a real pleasure to work with clients like Sandy, Bill, and a few others with equally desirable characteristics. I didn't do anything special to find these kinds of dream clients. We just connected at some point and found that we fit together well. I hope you'll be so fortunate. You might contemplate the characteristics you'd like to see in your own perfect clients so you can target your marketing efforts toward such folks and cultivate a long-term connection if you find one.

I've had a few other clients who rose above the norm in a different way: they actually paid me bonuses! After teaching a one-day class at one company, the payment I received included an extra five hundred dollars. When I inquired about this (I know, don't look a gift horse in the mouth), my contact said the feedback on my class was excellent and it made him look good. Hence, he thought I deserved a bonus. The same sort of thing happened with one or two other clients also. It's always great to know that people enjoy both the work you do and their relationship with you.

Alas, not all clients fit in this ideal class. The next two chapters describe some far less appealing clients and what you might do when certain problems arise.

Chapter 10

Clients Who Give You Grief

I have worked with about 130 clients in my years as a consultant and trainer, including companies in the United States and abroad, government agencies at the federal, state, and local levels, and individuals. I've sold my products to hundreds more customers worldwide. Nearly all of these have been easy and trouble-free to work with. But a few have given me headaches. This chapter relates some of the kinds of problems I've encountered so you can be alert for those in your own work as a consultant.

Getting stiffed

Several consultants I know have been stiffed by one or two of their clients—they simply never paid for services rendered. This has happened to me just once (see Chapter 17, "It's a Matter of Policy"). I've come close a couple of other times. I once did a two-week European seminar tour sponsored by a software tool vendor, teaching six one-day courses in three countries. Afterward, I could not get the company to pay me. It wasn't a trivial amount of money, either.

After multiple requests, I finally received a check. The check required the signatures of not one but two of the company's officers, yet no one at all had signed it! I'd had it. In a pretty sour mood, I called the company's president. A check for the full amount—signed, no less—arrived the next day. Amazing, eh? It just shouldn't be that difficult to get paid for the work you've done.

On two occasions, individual customers did not pay for some products they had ordered from me. They ignored my invoices and follow-up emails. As it happens, both of these customers were outside the United States. Consequently, I changed my billing policy. I will no longer ship a product to a purchaser outside the U.S. along with an invoice. Instead, I must receive payment before I will deliver the product. It's a shame that a very few people make life more difficult for everyone through their irresponsible actions.

I've occasionally had problems with delayed payments when a client required me to enter into a subcontracting arrangement with one of their established contractors. The contractor typically waits until the client pays them for my services before they will pass the funds along to me. This can add a month or more to the usual payment cycle.

Last year just such a contractor didn't pay me on time and wouldn't respond to my inquiries. No one at the state government agency for whom I had done the work seemed to have any influence over the contractor, whom they had already paid. It took several months of inquiring, cajoling, threatening, and escalating (I consulted with a contracts attorney), but I finally did get paid in a series of biweekly installments. This kind of income uncertainty is just one of the factors you need to get used to as an independent consultant.

I think the contractor was having some cash flow problems that led to the delayed payment. Now, I'm not an unreasonable man. If they had simply told me about the situation, we could have worked out a payment schedule without this level of acrimony and frustration. I'll never work as a subcontractor again, and I'll never work for that client again.

On the plus side, for the first time in my twenty-three-year consulting experience, I had to invoke the interest-due-on-late-payments clause that I include in every contract. Amazingly, that contractor paid the extra money without argument. So it turned out to be a good financial outcome for me, although it wasted a lot of my time, energy, and goodwill, and for a while I feared I wouldn't be paid at all.

Firing a client

When I worked at Kodak before I went independent I helped plan our internal software engineering conference one year. We had a speaker in mind for a keynote presentation, a well-known figure in a particular area of software engineering. However, one of the planning committee members reported that that consultant had had some previous unpleasant experience with Kodak, and he was no longer willing to work at the company. No one knew exactly what the details of the problem were.

At the time, my reaction was, "How arrogant!" When I became a consultant myself, however, I realized that some clients simply aren't worth the trouble. I've had a very few clients that I won't work with again for various reasons, including sluggish payments, too many problems encountered with contracting or invoicing (like invoices that disappeared simply because one particular individual changed jobs), and incredibly slow or erratic decision-making.

Obviously, if you need the income and the opportunity presents itself, you'll probably just bite your tongue and tolerate difficult clients. But if you have the luxury of having enough work, it sometimes makes sense to say, "Thanks, but no thanks" when certain clients call you again.

One of my consultant friends tried for nearly eighteen months to receive a payment from a very large technology company, to no avail. Ultimately, they offered to pay him a discounted amount within thirty days, or the entire balance at some indeterminate future date. Totally fed up, my friend contacted the office of the president of this huge company. To his delight, he got paid right away. Wouldn't it have been easier for everyone if they had just paid the bill as promised? My friend refused to do any further work with that client. Coincidentally, I've had so many problems with that same well-known company that years ago I decided not to deal with them again either. They just aren't worth it.

Problems with clients sometimes lead to changes in your business practices. When I encountered a couple of clients who took far longer than I thought was reasonable to pay me, I decided to establish a new policy. Rather than invoicing a new client after I deliver a training course for the speaking fee plus my travel and lodging expenses, I began quoting an all-inclusive fee, submitting an invoice in advance, and requesting that payment be delivered when I'm there to present the course.

Nearly all of my clients accepted this policy. I might relax the policy when I have a sustained and successful relationship with a client or in other special circumstances, like when I wish to defer income into the next calendar year for tax reasons. Otherwise, though, the class starts when I receive my check.

Some consultants request payment of a portion of their fee in advance, which they retain if the client cancels the event. I've never done that, although I do include a cancellation fee in my speaking agreement. See Chapter 16, "Everything's Negotiable," for more about cancellation fees.

Questionable ethics

I use a simple written consulting agreement to itemize the specifics of each client engagement. A prospective client once asked me to state in the agreement that I would be performing a certain kind of work, because that's what they had funding for. In reality, I would be doing something different after I arrived on site. My client told me that if the agreement stated what I would really be doing, his management wouldn't approve it.

This struck me as unethical. What if a senior manager had discovered that I was doing something other than what had been approved and funded? Not only would I probably not get paid, I wouldn't be hired by that company again, and my professional reputation could be damaged. I suppose I could even get sued.

There are a lot of gray areas when it comes to integrity. But if someone clearly asks you to lie about work that you do, that's pretty black-and-white. I declined this invitation and never dealt with that company again.

A poor fit

The notion of being scrupulously ethical in professional dealings applies to consultants as well as to clients, of course. While I was at Kodak early in my software development career, my team needed to bring in a database consultant from a major vendor for some short-term help. I spoke to the prospective consultant and asked how much experience he had in the area with which we were struggling.

"I haven't done that before," he replied, "but I can learn along with you." I'm sorry, that answer is incorrect, but thanks for playing. It seemed unethical for him to request that we pay $1,200 a day for him to learn alongside us. We found a different consultant.

As a consultant, it's important to acknowledge your limitations as well as your capabilities. Once in a while I receive an inquiry from a prospective client who's looking for help in an area in which I lack expertise. I never offer a proposal in such a case because I know there are more appropriate people available. If someone can do a better job for the client than I can for a particular service, that's who the client should hire. I'm always happy to refer a client to another consultant who's a better fit for their needs. Similarly, I'm grateful when other consultants point clients towards me.

I neither pay nor accept finder's fees for these sorts of referrals. I figure that if everybody is willing to help match up prospective clients with the right consultants, then everybody's back gets scratched. It all averages out in the end.

Knocking your head against the wall

A friend of mine whom I'll call Peter pointed out that when you've lost hope of having any effectiveness with a client, it's time to move on. You should also bail if a company is abusing or taking advantage of you in any way.

Peter once consulted for a company that practiced what he termed "management by rage." Peter made it clear to his contacts that there'd better not be any rage directed at him. The relationship worked for a while, but then Peter became viewed as a threat by a particular manager. One day that manager raged at Peter behind closed doors for twenty minutes, complaining, "You're trying to take over my job!" In reality, Peter had no interest in the manager's job. The man was simply being unreasonable. Peter did get the manager to apologize to him at one point during the meeting for making such outrageous statements.

Afterward, Peter was understandably shaken by the experience. After he calmed down, he thought about whether he still wanted to pursue that consulting engagement. He decided no, so he quit. The company's management sent a more reasonable person to see how much money Peter wanted to come back, but Peter still said no and walked away.

Again, a very few clients simply are not worth the aggravation they cause. Try to identify them early and make your escape.

Clients who go dark

I once had a client who brought me in twice, both to deliver some training classes and to do some consulting work. The events all went fine, and the manager who hired me seemed happy with the results. At the end of my second visit he said he wanted to set up another engagement soon.

After I returned home, I sent this manager a speaking agreement for the dates he had requested. No reply. I emailed him several more times to follow up. No answer. I phoned and left several voice mails. No response.

This client literally never contacted me again. I don't know what the problem was, but I would have appreciated it had he simply told me they were no longer interested in my services. This would have saved me the time and trouble of repeatedly attempting to contact him, which I was doing at his request, after all. Weird.

Actually, I did hear from him a few years later, in a way. I received a flood of virus-infested emails that apparently came from his email address. Somehow, that seemed fitting.

Chapter 11

Difficult Client? Try these Quick Tips

Contributed by Margaret Meloni

> Margaret Meloni, MBA, PMP is the pmStudent.com community leader. pmStudent.com is devoted to helping you successfully navigate the art and science of project management. Her background in IT project management and PMO leadership enables Margaret to understand the challenges you face in managing projects. A recipient of the UCLA Extension Distinguished Instructors award, her wish is to see her students take on tough projects and emerge as strong and sought-after project managers.

Your hands are sweating; your stomach is in knots. Once again, you have a client who has become truly obnoxious. Somehow, he is driving you crazy. If you say left, he says right. The hiring honeymoon is over, and now you see that your client is—believe it or not—a difficult person.

Part of your challenge is that your attachment to your client is both financial- and relationship-based. Oh, and it is tied to money. Wait, did I already say that? Well, which of you are NOT in business to make money?

What about being respected for your knowledge and your expertise? And—dare I say it—what about your ego? How can this person, this client, hire you to do something and then turn around and disregard your advice? Or, even worse, ask for your input and then do the exact opposite? I mean, really, what's up with that?

You know that your reputation either attracts or repels potential clients. You also know that your ability to get along well with your clients is a strong component of your professional reputation. I would suggest that most of the burden of resolving a difficult situation resides with you. As a consultant, you are hired to be the best of the best. Frequently you serve as a role model to your client and their team. There are expectations that come with being hired for your skills and experience; you are expected to represent professional behavior at its very best.

It is not likely that your difficult client will change for you, but you can change the way the two of you interact. You can take more control of the situation and work toward a positive outcome. To accomplish that, I must ask you to do two things: let go of your attachment to finances, and, if applicable, set your ego aside.

When you let money and ego drive the situation, it shows. I recently overheard a consultant speaking about one of his clients in this manner. "I do not have time for their problems; I have money to make," the consultant said. I'll bet his client thinks of HIM as the difficult person. Unless this consultant has some very rare expertise, this might not be a long-term assignment, and this client probably will not look to him for future engagements. However, this doesn't mean that if you *do* have rare expertise, it's okay to be difficult. No one enjoys dealing with difficult people.

If you can let your concern for building an effective working relationship take charge, you are well on your way to a positive outcome. Once you're ready to speak to your difficult client about the friction points, consider the following approach.

- Prepare for the conversation in advance. Identify what you hope to gain from the interaction, and begin with this end in mind.
- Be flexible. Do not be so focused on your end goal that you can't take a detour in the conversation. This detour may help you better understand your difficult client's point of view.

- Select a time that is convenient for both of you, a time when you both can listen and exchange ideas.
- Listen—really listen—to what your difficult client has to say. If he says something like, "I cannot do that" or "That won't work," ask why. Whatever issue he has might not be about you at all. Try to get the real problem out in the open.
- Consider letting the client speak first. If he seems comfortable taking the lead in the conversation, let him.
- Maintain emotional objectivity. Remember, whatever drives him to be difficult is about him, not about you. Again, try to turn off your ego and stop thinking about your checkbook.
- Stay calm. An individual who is upset may become defensive and verbally attack you. If this happens, take a deep breath and pause before responding.

If the discussion becomes too heated, you might suggest to your difficult client that you both take some time to cool off. Then agree upon a time when you will reconvene.

No matter how challenging, you both need to resolve the issue. Create an agreement between you and your client to stick with the situation until you have both been able to understand one another. You want to create a relationship where you and your difficult client can respect each other as individuals and professionals, even if you'll never be best friends.

Chapter 12

The Challenges and Adjustments of Remote Consulting

Contributed by Joan Davis

> *Joan Davis (J Davis Consulting, LLC) is a specialist in collaborative discovery, helping businesses and educational institutions create roadmaps to navigate change. Her background includes over twenty years as a business analyst and project manager, leading business and IT workgroups in problem solving, workflow design, and prioritizing business requirements. Joan now provides facilitated business analysis for clients who want to create engaging group experiences that improve communication and teamwork, with added value to distributed operations as an expert practitioner of the techniques and technologies of virtual collaboration. Reach Joan at https://www.linkedin.com/in/jdavisconsulting.*

It's a miracle that I get work at all. When my neighbors in Maine learn that I conduct virtual meetings for a living, they look at me quizzically and then look away. Phone conversations with prospective clients include long pauses when they find out I'll be working pretty much from home. There's some awkward emailing of contracts and statement-of-work revisions. Somewhere along the way to agreement, there's an introductory long-distance conversation with key stakeholders. Usually I must prove my stuff in this one virtual meeting. That's just to get to the point where we start working together at a distance.

Yet I'm making some small headway, and I'm encouraged when Karl tells me he's operated remotely for years. When I moved here a few years ago, my location forced a transition completely away from traditional on-site consulting. Since then, my work as a virtual business analyst and facilitator has had its ups and downs. There's a certain expectation in my field that workshops will be facilitated from the front of a roomful of people. Maybe in your own consulting work you encounter the same resistance about performing your activities off-site and away from the clients.

I've adapted my face-to-face consulting approach and now specialize in virtual collaboration. Whether you work remotely or you're partnered on-site with a distributed team, these practices could improve your virtual collaboration efforts.

Facing the challenges

You face a special blend of risks when you're working off-site. The challenges have to do with assumptions about the critical nature of face time for the consulting partnership.

Relationship building. Working at a distance prohibits coffee breaks together or meeting up socially after work, so how will you build those important alliances?

Communication strategy. As an outpost worker you must make sure you don't fall off the grid, out of sight and out of touch. How will you ensure you're in the loop? How will you share information without deluging each other's inbox?

Common understanding. One of your greatest attributes as a consultant is sensing the client's reactions and being able to read between the lines. Without the benefit of body language and other visual cues, how will you ensure clarity on all sides?

Team engagement. With your team members in multiple locations, what steps will you take to ensure there is a rich, continuous, and conversational collaboration on the work that matters the most to success?

Five strategies for mastering remote engagement

The virtual collaboration message I give my customers is one of large-group innovation and cost savings. To forge my way in this professional space I've had to transform the way I interact with clients and project teams. Following are five strategies I use to address the challenges of virtual collaboration.

Open communication channels: adding a personal touch

I found that some amazing bonds originate with actions as small as initiating a one-on-one call or a video chat. Arrange time with each of your co-workers just to get to know them better. You'll be rewarded with fresh insights and with someone new in your corner, a tremendous asset for the virtual worker.

Once you've connected personally, finding the right tactics to stay in touch is important to the health of your working relationships. Respect schedules and communication preferences, while being responsive to changing needs. When dealing with global communications, give additional consideration to differences in technology access, culture, and time zones.

My consulting engagements are now guided by a virtual communications strategy that my distributed team derives collectively. It frames how we will conduct our key project interactions: exchange of critical information, reporting of autonomous activities, and timely notification of changes. For instance, I like to share my work-in-progress regularly. With the inherent lag time of asynchronous communications, I allow more time for a review cycle and seek feedback earlier than I did when working on-site. I prefer a pull rather than a push model for my stakeholders to stay informed, posting information updates to an online workspace rather than emailing status updates.

Asynchronous thinking: individual inputs and agreements over time

My tendency is to use live meetings as the hub of all collaborative activity. The groundwork of "inputs" is well established before the synchronous (live) part of the collaboration. Time together should not be wasted on sharing information that could have been done in advance. Asynchronous methods—Wikis, discussion threads, surveys, and the like—work well for collecting feedback and comments. With 95 percent of the groundwork already done prior to the meeting, my virtual collaborators can focus on the one or two key issues that are best resolved through real-time interaction. When we exit the live meeting a new asynchronous round begins.

Facilitated discussions: leading and listening

As I work virtually with the team on more structured tasks, I consider my role to be a facilitator of distributed dialogue. It doesn't matter if there are two people or fifty in the conversation. Listening is an integral part of being a consultant, whether face-to-face or virtual. However, as a virtual team leader you *must* promote active listening: prompting, rephrasing, and using open-ended questions to ensure understanding.

When you are all working in the same physical room you might use flip charts to record ideas and sticky notes to organize consensus-building activities. Consider how you will hold ideas in the light for discussion with a distributed group. You have many options to draw or take notes online so your live collaborators all can see.

Uniform experience: activities balanced for local and remote participants

It's perhaps most difficult to strike a balance with hybrid meetings, when some participants are in the same room while you and people in other outposts are participating remotely. To encourage everyone to participate from their own desks, I set up the meeting process to require keyboard interactions that will keep them engaged with the group activities. If that's not possible and some participants will be face-to-face, just be sure to facilitate for the people who are remote, emphasizing verbal descriptions and calling on people by name.

[An aside from Karl: I once moderated a peer review of a requirements document remotely. All of the other participants sat in a room together at their company, while I was in my home office far away. Moderating a review meeting is a facilitation activity. It involves making sure that all attendees are engaged in the process and contributing constructively. The moderator must also control any inappropriate or ineffective interactions, such as distracting side conversations. Effective moderation often requires reading body language, such as noticing when someone might be starting to say something but hasn't quite got there yet.

I found it quite challenging to keep this meeting moving along productively when I could not see the other participants, whom I had never met. We did get through it and had a constructive outcome. It was quite a different experience from being able to look the others in the eye around the table though.]

Breakout sessions: live small-group work sandwiched by large-group dialogue

In a virtual meeting with larger groups, I rely on audio breakout sessions to ensure that everyone is engaged. Some teleconferencing tools enable private subgroup conversations with hosting features to customize groupings, drop in on conversations, and time the session. Set the stage with the full group of remote attendees to gain a sense of common purpose. Then charge subsets of participants with either the same or different tasks, as appropriate, and off to work they go.

At the designated time reconvene the full group to share their results. Posing problems for small groups to solve encourages everyone to interact, and regrouping the small teams creates an environment for building trust among distributed participants.

Collaboration tools

I have compiled a downloadable list of many of the available tools that I've found helpful for virtual consulting and other forms of long-distance collaboration. The tools are grouped into categories by the goal you're attempting to accomplish:

- Co-authoring a shared document
- Anonymous text-based input collection
- Virtual team online community platform
- Scheduling across time zones
- Phone and web conferencing
- Virtual breakout sessions
- Online whiteboard for live drawing

This list is available at the supplemental web page that accompanies this book, https://tinyurl.com/goingitalone. Tools and vendors come and go regularly, so use this list as a starting point to find the right tool for you.

Fulfilling the consulting promise

Virtual collaboration can bring success to widely dispersed groups who need to share ideas, knowledge, or project work, tapping into a global network of brainpower. My consulting portfolio now includes many communication techniques that help to engage and move virtual teams through a project. The way I influence change is to help the distributed team to reach agreement on actionable responses. Soon my clients come to accept that we really *don't* have to be in the same room to work together, because facilitated virtual dialogue solidifies my effectiveness from afar. Hallelujah!

Part 3

Practicalities

Chapter 13

What Are You Worth?

One of your first challenges as a self-employed person is determining what to charge for your various products and services. There isn't a guidebook for setting prices. It's very much a matter of what the market will bear. As with most services, the more experience you have and the better known you are in your field, the more you can charge. Some of the consultants I've known charge less than they could probably get away with. It's hard to know how much you can command until you push the limits and see what happens.

Happy either way

The best advice I ever found on setting prices came from a great book by Gerald Weinberg called *The Secrets of Consulting: A Guide to Giving & Getting Advice Successfully*. Weinberg's Principle of Least Regret states "Set the price so you won't regret it either way." In other words, choose a price so you're happy whether the client says yes or no to your proposal. I keep this principle in mind every time I prepare a price quote for a prospective engagement.

For instance, I have one course that I have taught, most often in two-day format, 187 times. Put another way, I have spent more than one full year of my life presenting this material! It's not very exciting for me anymore, although it is still in demand. If a client asks me to teach this course now, I often would rather not do it. Therefore, I might ask for more money to teach that course than for another one that's more interesting to do. If the client accepts my offer, fine—I'll be there. I'll do the best job I possibly can because that's what the students deserve, regardless of how I feel about it. I'll smile all the way to the bank.

Weinberg's principle also served as a good way to regulate how many commitments I made during those years when I was fortunate enough to receive an abundance of inquiries. If you're hungrier, you might be tempted to charge less to boost your chances of landing the gig. During the rich times, though, you can quote higher fees to make sure you don't exhaust yourself by accepting every possible opportunity that comes along. It's all a matter of balancing your supply of time with customers' demand for your services.

What the market will bear

When I launched my independent consulting career in the late 1990s, I set my prices based on what I saw other experienced consultants were charging. Back then I charged $1,500 a day for consulting and $2,500 a day for training. I figured that training was a higher-leverage activity. The client received more value per day when I was delivering useful information to twenty-five students at a time than in a one-on-one consultation. Therefore, I believed I was entitled to more compensation.

Over the years, those rates went up. But I still know some established consultants who are charging only around $1,500 a day to deliver training. In my view, they are underpricing their services. Obviously, you'll make less if you're working through a parent company that contracts out your services or an agency that finds jobs for you. They're working on your behalf and are entitled to their slice.

There is a school of thought that says the higher your price, the greater the perception of value to the prospective client. Therefore, you will get more work if you charge more. Sometimes this strategy does work, at least up to a point. I have some colleagues who said they landed more gigs when they raised their training rate. Of course, there's an upper cap beyond which prospective clients will seek lower-priced options.

I've done some experiments with pricing the products I sell through my website, such as e-learning courseware and template collections. I wanted to test this notion that increasing the price also increases the perceived value, thereby leading to more sales. I've tried raising prices, lowering prices, running half-price sales, offering discounted bundle packages, and offering buy-one-get-one-free promotions. Nothing seems to make much difference in how many items I sell. I've concluded that if someone wants a particular product, they're likely to just buy it, if the price is not totally out of line. They're not going to buy something they're not enthusiastic about, no matter the price.

If more competitors enter your domain, this can exert downward price pressure. I observed this in the field of software requirements. I got into the game early, with a well-received book and numerous articles and presentations in this area. I could command substantial training fees. However, as more and more people wrote books about requirements and business analysis and developed their own training materials, requirements training became more of a commodity. I couldn't quote the same fees and still be competitive, although certain clients did want me personally to teach the class because I wrote the textbook. Again, it's all about what the market will bear.

Partway through my career I began offering a service of off-site consulting at an hourly rate that works out to less than my usual daily on-site consulting rate. This way I can provide useful services to clients who perhaps don't wish to spend a lot of money, have just a few questions or a small project, only want me to review some documents for them, or seek a little coaching on specific topics. I've even conducted large-scale and long-term engagements like this for remote clients, which has worked out well for everyone.

Most of my consulting work over the past several years has been done in this off-site fashion. I don't have to travel, I can work in my pajamas if I like, and I can work however many hours per day I wish so long as I meet the client's deadlines. This hourly rate reduces a new client's risk. They don't need to buy an entire day and hope they'll get their money's worth.

I suggest you base your price for a specific engagement on the value you're providing to the client. Delivering a presentation with an unlimited audience provides more value to the client than a class with restricted attendance. If I'm helping one person with some project questions, I will probably provide less value than if I'm developing a new requirements process to be deployed across the company's development organization.

You want fries with that?

I often present a client with the option to bundle multiple services or products at a discounted price. If they're bringing me in to teach a class, I might offer to provide a certain amount of follow-up consulting to help them leverage the investment they're making in the training for maximum benefit. A colleague refers to this sort of enhancement offer as "fries."

As another example, I typically offer a hefty discount on the purchase of an e-learning course site license after I present a live class at the client's location. My standard proposal for e-learning courses offers bundle discounts like 10 percent off any two courses purchased at once and 20 percent off three or more courses purchased together. Basically, once I have a client who recognizes the value I can provide to her organization, I make sure she knows about all the resources I have available. There might be more money lurking in the client's budget that I can tap into.

It's important to keep in mind the objective of a win-win outcome. Most of the time, a client and a consultant can agree upon a fee structure that satisfies all of the participants and seems fair to everyone. If you can't, walk away.

Chapter 14

Money Matters for the New Consultant

Contributed by Gary K. Evans

Gary K. Evans is an independent agile consultant. He has spent two decades helping Fortune 500 companies incorporate agile methods and object-oriented techniques. He is a Certified Scrum Master, an Agile Coach, and a SAFe 4 Program Consultant.

You probably didn't become a consultant as a hobby. You're looking to make a living from it, which means you need to deal with money. This chapter addresses some of the economic practicalities of running your business, as either a self-employed independent consultant or a free-lance hourly contractor.

First, hire an accountant

If you're a professional, I assume that you're very good at what you do. Because your area of expertise probably doesn't include accounting and tax regulations, you should hire a fellow professional—an accountant—to take care of these matters. Make sure to shop around and find one with at least some self-employed clientele.

Like technologists and any other professional, accountants differ in their skills and specialties. My accountant makes more per hour than I do, and he's worth every penny. Each year, he has saved me money that would have otherwise slipped through my fingers.

Some consultants prefer to prepare their own tax returns, so they buy Intuit QuickBooks or an equivalent tool to help them track their business income and business expenses. I certainly would not criticize this—I use QuickBooks myself. Whether or not you enlist the services of a professional accountant, you must keep meticulous track of your finances. QuickBooks does this. It will generate invoices for your clients, flag receivables that are past their due date, and so forth. If you try to do this with Excel, you are more adventurous than I. Spring for the money to buy a proper tool like QuickBooks. It's a deductible business expense, and you will be very glad you did. So will your accountant, if you have to provide a categorized general ledger file so you can claim the proper deductions and depreciations at tax time.

A relationship with an accountant can also be helpful when you have to make estimated federal and state income tax payments. Unlike corporate employment, where taxes are withheld from each paycheck, self-employed people must pay their own estimated taxes to the Internal Revenue Service. To make your life harder, these payment periods are not of uniform length. Due dates are January 15, April 15, June 15, and September 15, pushed back as necessary for weekends and holidays. You can mail in the payments or pay online with the Electronic Federal Tax Payment System®.

If you are reasonably skilled at preparing your own tax returns, you can estimate these necessary payments yourself. Otherwise, enlist your accountant to help. There are penalties for substantial underpayments of estimated taxes and for late payments. It can be difficult to guess correctly at the amount of tax due if your income is erratic throughout the year, as it typically is for an independent consultant. It's just one more of the complications you face when you go it alone.

Rates: Don't be a cheap date

Setting rates is neither a science nor a crapshoot. You can peruse some of the many books on this topic to learn exactly how to do this, whether you do fixed fee, daily rate, or hourly rates. Karl offered some suggestions on setting rates in Chapter 13, "What Are You Worth?" Here, I'll comment only on some of the pitfalls I've personally encountered.

You don't work every day. Regular employees get up in the morning, go to work, and come home in the evening. Every day. An independent consultant or a contractor gets up every morning, but what happens after that is somewhat random. In a good economy, expect to be unemployed about a quarter of each year. You do want to have some kind of life, don't you?

Another way to think of this is that you work three weeks and have no engagement the fourth week of each month. Factor this down time into your price setting. And, in a bad economy, prepare for up to six months without work. In my worst year, I worked only four months out of twelve. It was tough, but my past discipline in setting aside savings got us through.

Should you match the going rate? Finding the going rate for, say, C#/.NET developers in Washington, D.C., or anywhere else is easy. The internet is the most accessible source of such information. Recruiting companies often publish salary surveys organized by skill and geographical region. Starting out, be aware of what clients are paying both salaried employees and contractors. Independent contractors must cover business expenses that employees don't have, so they're expected to request hourly-equivalent rates from 40 to 100 percent higher than do regular employees—but you do have to be good enough to justify these higher rates.

I've found considering your value to be a tremendous factor in determining your consulting rates. Value is often equated with price, and I'm not the first person to note that when I increased my rates, I got more and better work because my perceived value increased. If you have extensive experience and real expertise, you can command higher rates.

Lowering your rate to get work. This is a disaster, both now and for the future. Small clients all want to get top-quality workers for $25 to $35 per hour. If you're willing to go that low just to work, I urge you to get a corporate job that pays the same rate and comes with some benefits.

Paying your own expenses from your daily or hourly pay. I did this once—for four weeks. Never again. Now I bill the client for my services and invoice separately for my expenses, perhaps up to an agreed-upon maximum amount. I don't even negotiate on any other arrangement. Unless you're bidding on a fixed-fee project, reputable companies who work with independents expect to pay services and expenses separately.

However, this is just my policy. Karl has approached this issue rather differently than I. He quotes fixed rates for short on-site training engagements that include a portion to cover reasonable hotel, travel, and meal expenses. His clients like this because it simplifies processing the invoices, as no receipts are required. And it gives Karl the flexibility to stay in a luxury hotel or sleep in a tent, depending on his choice. That approach also simplifies matters if the trip involves events for multiple clients, where individual expenses would otherwise have to be prorated among the clients.

Non-billable time. I was stunned when I discovered how much time I spent doing invoices and expense reports, cold calling and warm calling, organizing files and contact lists, learning new technology, and developing new material—and I couldn't bill anyone for the time! Estimates vary, but an independent consultant or contractor should plan to spend 20 to 30 percent of his working week in non-billable time.

The 2X/3X rule. Independent consulting is costly because you have to cover all your own expenses. That means you must consider yourself as an employer and price yourself with the mindset of an employer selling your services to a client at a rate that ensures a respectable profit margin. To this end, I offer up the 2X/3X rule, another piece of wisdom I received from a successful consultant.

First, identify the amount you'd be paid as a salaried employee at a corporation doing what you do as a consultant. Doubling this number will provide you a break-even target as a consultant. But if you triple your salary figure, you'll be able to reinvest in your business and grow it. When I first started out and determined the doubled figure, I almost choked. But after just a couple of years, I learned how right my more experienced colleague was.

There are roughly two thousand working hours in a year, so a before-tax employee salary of $100,000 equates to $50 per hour. A consultant doing the same work as an employee earning $100,000 should be asking for $100 to $150 per hour. Why? The consultant will probably work for a few weeks or months, and short-term engagements carry a higher hourly rate. The independent consultant has no employment security and must pay his or her own overhead: life and disability insurance, business liability insurance, retirement funding, computer equipment, maintenance and repairs, office supplies, telephones . . . That is why the 2X guideline only brings you to the breakeven point.

Don't burn cash on an office

I was amused by a colleague who decided he should go into independent consulting and immediately spent $5,000 on a laptop, fax machine (it was a while ago), new PC, answering machine (a long while ago), preprinted business forms with his color logo, and a bucket of really marginal items. And he didn't yet have a single client or even the prospect of one.

I suggest you build an office as you need one. When I started consulting twenty-five years ago, I bought an answering machine first so I'd be able to return calls. When my first client called to say he had selected me and was faxing me a contract, I asked him to delay sending it until after lunch. Then I ran out and bought my first fax machine and hooked it up. I received the contract, signed it, and faxed back the signature page. That machine lasted seven years, but it had to pay its own way first.

Sole proprietorship versus incorporation

This is an important issue. Incorporating gives you some legal and financial protection, but it incurs costs, such as extra accounting and filing fees, among others. Some people incorporate right away (presumably an S corporation designation, not a C corporation like Fortune 100 companies). Others wait to incorporate until they have an established business and want to shelter their income. Part of the issue is image: corporations have a cachet of stability. Another part is cultural: some companies won't hire a sole proprietor and work only with corporations.

Another option is to set up a limited liability company or LLC. This is a business structure that is simpler and less expensive than an S corporation, still allows money to flow directly to the LLC organizers (that is, you), and presents a more business-like image than being a sole proprietor.

I was a sole proprietor under the DBA (doing business as) designation for more than six years before I incorporated as an S corporation. I now have a second business for software product development, set up as an LLC. The structure you choose is a business and legal decision. You should listen to your accountant and legal advisers for guidance on the structure that is best for you, your goals, and the financial risk exposure associated with the kinds of work you do.

Planning for retirement

As a self-employed person, you're also responsible for planning for your family's financial security after you retire. Perhaps you're already skilled at navigating the befuddling world of investments. If not, look for a fee-only financial planner to help you set up appropriate retirement accounts.

Beyond traditional and Roth individual retirement arrangements (IRAs), sole proprietors and those who have incorporated can set aside additional money in accounts such as a SEP-IRA or various types of pension plans. There are all sorts of tax implications, maximum contribution limits, and other issues with retirement planning that cry out for professional guidance. It's complicated, and there can be very significant long-term implications if you choose poorly.

Don't put this off. It's too important.

Chapter 15

Get It In Writing

I confess: I'm a process kind of guy. Recognizing that memories are imperfect and details can easily become lost, I like to write down important information so everyone involved in some activity knows what's happening and agrees to the plan. For this reason, I record the particulars of significant agreements I make with clients to avoid confusion, mistakes, and hard feelings. In this chapter I'll describe some of those agreements. You can download templates for the various sorts of simple agreement documents I've created from https://tinyurl.com/goingitalone.

Speaking agreement

I've spent much of the past two decades traveling to companies and government agencies around the world to deliver training courses. I always use a simple speaking agreement for these events. This agreement contains information such as:

- The particulars of the event, including location, the maximum number of attendees, dates and times, and contact person
- Instructions for setting up the room and my needs for the facility, such as a projector for my laptop, flip charts with easels and markers, and a lavalier microphone
- Information about the student handouts and textbooks we will use

- Financial details, including my money-back guarantee
- Contingencies for unexpected occurrences that could disrupt the event, including cancellation and rescheduling fees

This information all fits on one page. It works just fine for most engagements. However, sometimes the client's legal department wants to get involved. They always create a vastly longer and more complex contract that we have to negotiate. It took a full month to work through issues on the last such client agreement I had to deal with, although that was unusually long. I like my simple template much better.

This agreement has worked well for me for years. I never undertake an engagement without one. I won't make travel arrangements or order books until I've received a signed speaking agreement back from the client. Otherwise, I'm not confident they have fully committed to the event and the date. Several prospective clients never returned the agreement for an event they had requested. It's frustrating for me to have to hold those dates open and keep checking back to see if the client wishes to proceed.

I have a consultant friend who loathes paperwork. He never uses a written agreement with his clients if he can get away without one. Luckily, he hasn't encountered any problems with this approach—yet. But I've had some experiences for which having a written agreement was quite valuable; other consultants have shared similar stories with me.

One time I traveled to the New Jersey countryside to teach a three-day class at a large company. The next morning I went to the building where the class was to be held. No one was there to meet me. I finally reached my contact person on the phone. She thought the class was going to begin the *next* day and run for three days. Ah, that explained why the receptionist didn't know what I was talking about.

I pulled out the speaking agreement—I always take it with me. Sure enough, I was there on the correct date. By not reading the agreement carefully, my contact had miscommunicated to all the students in the class. We now had only two days to cover everything we were originally going to cover in three. If I had shown up a day late for a class I was supposed to teach, I'm sure there would have been financial consequences, not to mention the inconvenience to all the students. In this case, we were able to work it out, but it was a mistake that didn't have to happen.

Consulting agreements

I use two different templates for consulting—as opposed to training—engagements, one for work performed at the client site and the other for work I do at home. I call this second sort of activity off-site consulting; others might call it virtual or remote consulting. You can find the templates that I use for both kinds of engagements at https://tinyurl.com/goingitalone.

My template collection includes an alternative on-site consulting agreement template (#2) that was contributed by a colleague. This one is a little more formal and richer in legal details than mine, which might be a good idea. If you need to create such templates for your own consulting business, I suggest you study these and any other examples you can locate from experienced colleagues, then pull together the best ideas from all of them to suit your situation.

When I have an established long-term relationship with a client, I might not bother to write an agreement for a specific engagement. I have one such client at a company with whom I've worked for a long time. We work together very well, and I never have to worry about him not paying me or encountering some other misunderstanding. In a case like this, I dispense with the written agreements as an unnecessary overhead step. See, I'm a pragmatic—not dogmatic—process weenie.

Courseware licensing agreement

In keeping with my general business philosophy of trying to earn a living while I'm asleep, many years ago I began licensing my courseware to other companies. Some of these are themselves training companies or independent consultants, who can deliver my classes to their own clients and pay me a royalty when they do.

Other licensees are companies or government agencies that wish to use my materials for internal presentations, employing their own staff as instructors.

I have crafted licensing agreements for these two different situations. Again, you may access my templates for the licensing agreements at https://tinyurl.com/goingitalone. These agreements specify the materials I'm providing, the licensing fees and payment terms, and how the licensee may and may not use the materials.

I should point out that the terms in my various templates are not cast in concrete. Periodically, a prospective client or licensee raises particular concerns or has a situation that's a little out of the ordinary. They might ask me to adjust some of the terms. Sometimes, making that adjustment is the difference between closing a deal and not. So I certainly have some negotiating flexibility in portions of these agreements.

But there are limits. For instance, I will never remove the cancellation or rescheduling fee clause from my speaking agreement, although I might agree to adjust my initial terms if the client pushes back in a reasonable way. Also, I never license courseware to a company without some payment up front. That would essentially be giving away my content for free, something I just don't do.

The usual disclaimer

Although I have used these agreements for many years without any problems, they may or may not be suitable for you. I recommend you have an attorney look over whatever agreement templates you create to make sure they cover all the important bases and provide you with adequate protection, while still being fair to the client.

Most of the time, a well-crafted and simple agreement suffices to establish the parameters of your client engagements so both parties know what to expect. I do feel better having it in writing.

Chapter 16

Everything's Negotiable

In the previous chapter I described the simple agreements I use to record all the details for each of my speaking and consulting engagements. These usually work fine, but occasionally I will get some pushback from the client on specific terms in the agreement. Sometimes, the client's legal department rejects my simple agreement and sends me a massive document to sign.

But I don't just sign that contract. A contract is naturally written to the benefit of the entity that created it, so you need to watch out for any terms that are unacceptable to you. I read the contract carefully, looking for anything that makes me uncomfortable. I have discovered that many of the terms in a boilerplate contract can be adjusted if you aren't happy with them.

I'm in the midst of such a negotiation this very day. So far, this client is proving quite flexible on my requested changes. For instance, the client's standard services contract demanded that I take a drug test, something I've encountered only once before. I explained that I don't take drugs, and I don't take drug tests. The client dropped the requirement. Sometimes you just have to ask.

But in the earlier situation, that other client decided not to hire me to teach a class because I declined to take their drug test. Some years later I discovered that, instead, they had hired one of my licensees to come into the city where I lived and teach my class. That instructor, who happened to be Canadian, told me the client never asked him about taking a drug test! Some things just make no sense at all.

Following are some typical categories where you might need to negotiate with a client to agree upon a mutually acceptable contract.

Fees

The most obvious negotiable term is the fee you're requesting for your services. Frankly, I've found that clients don't challenge this as frequently as I expected. I have standard rates that I quote for certain services, but there's some flexibility in them. I'll offer a nice discount if a client wants to acquire a site license for some of my e-learning training courses in addition to having me present a live class. I'll also drop the price if the client wants a combination of consulting and training services or requests multiple presentations during the same trip.

Once, a prospective client asked for a discount of several thousand dollars off a two-day training course simply because my quote exceeded her budget. She said she just wanted me to knock the price down because I'm such a nice guy. Sorry, I'm not *that* nice. I wasn't willing to do the job for the price she suggested, and we never did come to an agreement. That's the way some negotiations turn out.

Cancellation

My speaking agreements always include a fee for canceling or rescheduling the event. Some clients balk at this. My premise is that, when I sign the agreement, I am committing a certain number of days for the client event, plus preparation and travel time. Should the client decide to change the agreed-upon date or to cancel the event entirely, it's unlikely that I can re-book that time slot with another client on short notice. If I purchase a nonrefundable airline ticket or have some books shipped to the client, changing the date or canceling the event will cost me money and inconvenience.

Therefore, I ask the client to make a similar commitment to me in the form of agreeing to pay me 20 or 25 percent of the price as a cancellation or rescheduling fee. Sometimes we negotiate a lower such fee. Or, we might put some time bounds around it. Maybe no payment is due if I can reschedule at no cost to me or if they cancel at least X weeks prior to the event. If the client does need to reschedule and it doesn't inconvenience me or cost me out of pocket, I will generally waive the rescheduling fee. But I always insist on including some language about rescheduling and cancellation fees in our agreement. If the client isn't willing to sign up for that, we don't make a deal.

One client tried waiting until immediately prior to the scheduled event to sign the speaking agreement, to minimize the likelihood of having to cancel or reschedule, thereby incurring a fee. However, my policy is to not commit specific dates to a client until I receive the signed speaking agreement. I felt no qualms about giving that client's requested date to another who was willing to make the commitment. I didn't appreciate the game of schedule chicken this client was playing with me. That gig ultimately fell through.

I've only had to invoke the cancellation or rescheduling fee four times during my career. Ironically, those invoices were all paid faster than my regular invoices. Go figure.

Usage rights

The boilerplate consulting-service contracts that some corporations use attempt to claim unreasonably broad rights for the presentation materials used in a training course. They might stipulate that the client has a perpetual free license to use the course materials in any way they wish, simply because I taught it once at their company. In principle, this right could extend to unlimited distribution of the material throughout the company, teaching the class themselves within or outside their company using those materials, posting the materials publicly on the internet, or even licensing my courseware to other companies without my knowledge or permission.

This is the first clause I ask to remove from every such service contract. My clients do not have the right to use my training materials for any purpose other than the courses I am presenting myself, unless we execute a separate licensing agreement. I've never had any problem getting this clause removed.

Video recording

Occasionally, a client asks to record my presentation and show it to other people throughout their company. This represents a lost revenue opportunity for me, because they might use the video rather than hiring me to come in and teach another class.

I am not totally averse to video recording. If my session is open to anyone in the company who wants to come, it's fine with me if they record it for anyone who couldn't attend the live session. Usually, though, my training courses are capped at a certain number of attendees for the agreed-upon fee. If they want to make a recording available to other people, I will generally permit this but charge them a little extra for the privilege.

Insurance

Contracts coming out of the legal department stipulate the various types of insurance the consultant is expected to carry. If your company has multiple employees, you might be required to provide workers' compensation insurance coverage. To my knowledge, though (and remember, this book contains no legal advice), sole proprietors with no employees are exempt from carrying workers' comp. Make sure to check your state laws on this.

I do carry business liability insurance, which offers some protection if, say, I injure a student with my laser pointer or damage client property with my rental car. If the coverage amounts stipulated in the contract are higher than I carry, I request to lower those coverage expectations to match my policy limits. Such requests have always been approved.

Some clients request to be listed as a named insured on your business liability insurance policy. This is easily accomplished with a phone call or email to your insurance agent.

I do not carry professional liability or malpractice (errors and omissions) insurance, although some companies request that. Clients have always been willing to remove that requirement when I point out that I don't carry it and that I don't need E&O coverage for the sorts of engagements I perform. Refer to Chapter 18, "For

Your Protection," for more information about insurance concerns for the independent consultant.

Other expenses

Today, for the first time in my career, a client required that I undergo a criminal background investigation. I have no objection to that, so long as they don't find out about all my secret offshore bank accounts or the yachts, but they wanted to charge me $49.79 for the privilege of being investigated. I persuaded the client to cover this unexpected cost.

That's the way most negotiations go. I agree to something the client is requesting, but then I issue a request of my own of comparable magnitude. We both feel as though the other party is being reasonable and flexible, which makes us amenable to reciprocating.

Today's client also asked about pulling a credit report on me. Also fine, if peculiar, as they will be paying *me* money, not the reverse. However, I have security freezes on my credit accounts with the three major consumer reporting agencies as protection against identity theft. If someone needs a credit report from me, I would have to pay ten dollars per agency to temporarily unfreeze my account. (The costs and conditions for placing, temporarily removing, and permanently removing a security freeze vary by state.) I asked the client to pay for that also, but they decided they didn't need to do a credit check after all. What a surprise.

Each party involved in a negotiation is striving to adjust the outcome in its own favor, but they should also respect their counterpart's legitimate needs. We all have limits to our flexibility. If the people with whom we're negotiating insist on finalizing the terms beyond our tolerance limits, we won't reach a mutually acceptable outcome. You don't win every negotiation, but you might be able to do better than you expect just by asking. I will sometimes give in on a minor point during a negotiation to resolve a point I feel more strongly about in my favor.

For more on effective negotiation, I highly recommend *Getting to Yes: Negotiating Agreement Without Giving In* by Roger Fisher, William Ury, and Bruce Patton. This book provides excellent advice on how to successfully negotiate from an understanding of each party's interests, rather than by passionately defending immovable positions.

As an aside, Chapter 24 of my book *Pearls from Sand* describes many ways I've been able to negotiate better deals in daily life. Just by asking in the right way I've saved money on shoes, delivering a treadmill to my house, magazine subscription renewals, cable TV bills, satellite radio for my car, medical services, clothing, landscaping services, and much more. The tips in that chapter alone will more than make up for the book's purchase price.

Chapter 17

It's a Matter of Policy

Every organization operates according to a set of policies, or business rules, whether explicitly documented or merely integrated into the culture's oral tradition. You should adopt policies for your consulting practice too. This chapter presents many operating policies I've accumulated for my one-person consulting and training company, Process Impact, as well as some I've heard from other consultants. I encourage you to formulate your own analogous policies.

On traveling

A central aspect of being a consultant or trainer is that you usually have to go where the work is. This isn't always true today, thanks to virtual consulting, webinar, and online collaboration technologies; see Chapter 12, "The Challenges and Adjustments of Remote Consulting," for more on this. Much of the time, though, you can expect to have to travel to client sites.

Early in my consulting career I had no idea how much work I was going to get, so I gratefully accepted every opportunity that came along. I was fortunate to get traction with the business quickly. As a consequence, I was doing a LOT of traveling. My busiest travel year involved 137 flight segments. It didn't take me long to decide that I

> **Don't travel during more than three weeks of each month.**

This doesn't mean that I was gone three-quarters of the time, just that I might travel one or more days during three out of every four weeks. It's important to set time aside at home to get caught up, maintain relationships with family and friends, develop new training material or other content, write articles and books, and even relax and enjoy yourself (or so I've heard).

This policy also has helped keep me healthy. I have two consultant friends who became ill and couldn't fully recover for several months because their back-to-back travel commitments were so exhausting. The only thing worse than traveling a lot is traveling while you're sick. Leave time in your schedule to treat yourself well.

Along that same line, I find it very tiring to teach more than two days in a row. It's hard to be witty and charming, both on your feet and on your toes, for seven or eight hours, day after day. Therefore, if a client asks me to teach two sessions of a two-day class, I will

Take Wednesday off between a pair of two-day training sessions.

I might do some sightseeing, visit friends in the area, or take in a movie. My voice, my feet, and my disposition all benefit from the break. Of course, I don't charge the client for my expenses or time on the day off.

Anyone who travels a lot has had the experience of being stranded overnight—or longer—in an airport or at a nearby hotel. It happens, whether due to bad weather, mechanical problems, missed connections, or terrorist acts. I was stranded at a client site far from home for several days after 9/11. Another consultant friend was stuck in a distant city for more than two days after a canceled flight. There simply was no space available on numerous later flights to accommodate all the affected passengers. I don't worry much about such delays on my way home, but it can be disastrous on your journey to a gig. Therefore, I decided long ago that I would

Never take the last flight of the day to a client site.

I'd rather arrive several hours early than to miss the engagement because I'm in an airport hotel a thousand miles away.

It's unnerving to have to search for your destination early in the morning on the first day of a gig in an unfamiliar city. Traffic can be heavier or more confusing than you expected, and you might encounter construction delays. The meeting location could be cleverly hidden somewhere in a vast corporate campus, or parking might be problematic. Maybe even all of the above. So to avoid starting my day with excessive stress, my policy is to

Practice the drive from the hotel to the event location the prior evening.

I've only arrived late for an event once in my consulting career, heading into Jersey City from a hotel near Newark one morning. Who knew the highway to the Holland Tunnel into Manhattan would be so popular during rush hour? Everyone except me, apparently. I never again groped my way to an unfamiliar location without a dry run beforehand.

I've done some work outside North America, going to Europe a couple of times and taking several trips to Australia and New Zealand. This led me to my next traveling policy. Now I treat myself. I

Only fly across an ocean in business class or better.

Yes, it's expensive, and no, you don't get there any faster. But it certainly is a lot more comfortable. I arrive at my distant destination better rested and ready to work. I build the fees for business class airfare into the price quotes I provide to my overseas clients. If they are unwilling to pay the cost, that's no problem—I just thank them for their inquiry and stay home. Unless, that is, I really want to go anyway, in which case I'll pay the additional airfare myself or upgrade with frequent-flier miles.

I have a consultant friend who thrives on international travel. He and his wife are adventurous people who love to explore exotic locations. They really suck the marrow out of life. (I tried to suck the marrow out of life once, but I chipped a tooth on the bone.) I haven't adopted this policy myself, but Ken has decided to

Spend one extra day sightseeing for each time zone change.

So if Ken goes to someplace like China or India, he takes his wife along and they spend several extra days touring, hiking, camping, or whatever. This is not a bad way to see the world if you can afford the time and cost.

You know all those little bars of soap that hotels give you? I don't let the extras go to waste. Instead I

Collect unused hotel soaps and shampoo bottles and donate them to a homeless shelter.

Some people think it's unethical to "steal" soap you didn't use. I view the soap as part of what I'm paying for the hotel room, so it bothers me not one whit to take it with me. Over the years I've given hundreds of little bars of soap and bottles of shampoo to people who need them more than I—or the hotel—do.

Some years ago I figured out an interesting traveling trick. I learned how to

Leverage airline frequent-flier programs against each other.

At the time I concocted this scheme, I held second-tier premium frequent-flier status on United Airlines. I wrote to American Airlines, which flew on some of the same routes, and invited them to match my premium status on United. They didn't bump me up two frequent-flier levels, but they did bump me up one. "Hmm," I said to myself, "that was easy." The next year I tried it again, and it worked again. Then I mailed a copy of my new premium-level card on American to Delta and made them the same offer. Again, they took my bait.

I pulled off this scheme for several years, parlaying premium status on one airline into others and enjoying the ensuing benefits. It cost me only a few postage stamps. There was nothing underhanded about this—I was simply presenting each airline with a business offer. One year, I held premium status on four airlines without having earned any of them! The scheme didn't always work, and at the moment I don't have premium status on any airline because I don't fly that much anymore. It was great while it lasted though.

Another trick I learned is to exploit the fact that prices for hotels, flights, and rental cars change frequently. Now I will

> **Check the prices for hotel rooms and rental cars I've already reserved before I leave.**

If a lower price is available, I simply call the hotel or rental car company and they readily change my reservation to the lower rate. I can find better rates this way roughly half the time.

Recently I performed this check for five hotels and a rental car I had reserved for a vacation coming up soon. With fifteen minutes of effort, I saved more than sixty dollars off three of my original reservations. I checked again the day before I left and saved almost thirty dollars more. It's worth the few minutes it takes to look.

On finances

In Chapter 13, "What Are You Worth?," I said that one of the most helpful tricks I learned about consulting was to

> **Set my price so I'm happy whether the client says yes or no.**

I have a standard daily training fee, which I adjust based on numerous factors for a given situation. I might knock the price down a bit if the destination is someplace I want to go anyway or if the gig sounds interesting. I'll quote a higher fee if I'm not that interested in the job or if the travel required is inconvenient. Most of the time that high price scares the client away. If not, then I'll sigh, get on the airplane, and cash the big check at the end.

One consultant I know was invited to travel from the east coast of the United States to Asia to deliver a half-day presentation. Not wanting to spend that much time traveling for such a short gig, he requested an outrageous fee and first-class airfare. The client agreed; off he went.

Partway through my career I also decided to

> **Quote an all-up fee that includes my expenses.**

This way I don't have to provide receipts that are potentially subject to client pushback for travel and lodging expenses, textbooks, printing student handouts, and the like. This policy has greatly simplified my invoicing.

Knowing the final price for an event up front also permits me to submit an invoice to the client in advance and to

Request payment at the time of the event.

I adopted this practice after having a ridiculous number of invoices get "lost" in clients' accounting systems. Getting paid right away reduces my aggravation level and saves me the time of chasing down late payments. I also do not let clients get away with their occasional attempts to give themselves a discount for payment within ten, or maybe even thirty, days. My standard terms are net thirty days, with no discount for early payment and an interest charge of 1 percent per month for late payment, which I waive if it's just a bit late. Some clients request forty-five days for payment. I'm okay with that, but I'll push back if they ask for sixty or more days.

One of my colleagues insists that

New clients outside the United States must pay half the fee in advance.

This is a good idea in case you have any concerns at all about whether you're going to get paid, in what currency, in what form, and when. A Canadian friend told me that he suffered a significant loss because of changing currency exchange rates, thanks to a client company in the United States that dragged its feet on payment. Of course, that could have gone the other way too, with exchange rates evolving in his favor. You never know with currency exchange rates.

Just this past week I had an experience that caused me to contemplate a new business policy. I had delivered a webinar at the invitation of a small company that sells certain software development tools. My invoice wasn't paid on time. When I followed up I learned that the company had just gone out of business. I am never going to get paid. So now I need to consider whether to ask small companies with potentially dodgy finances to pay me in advance for any work I do.

Early in my consulting career I was invited to speak at a meeting of a local professional society chapter. The contact person asked me what my fee would be. Not having done this sort of event before, I wasn't sure how to answer. However, after I thought about it, I concluded that I

> **Do not charge a fee to speak at a local meeting of a professional organization.**

I might request to have any travel expenses reimbursed, but I don't charge anything for the presentation itself. Delivering such presentations is a way for me to contribute to my profession, as well as being a marketing and networking opportunity. Conversely, I

> **Do not provide services to a company for free.**

A big company invited me to travel from my home in Portland, Oregon, to their site in Atlanta, Georgia, to present a ninety-minute lunch-and-learn session to their business analysts. They couldn't pay me, although they offered to reimburse my airfare. I'm astonished that people think any established consultant would be willing to spend nearly two days on cross-country travel without compensation. I declined, but I always appreciate the invitation. It means that people are interested in my work.

Companies sometimes invite consultants and authors to speak for free, arguing that it is a good advertising opportunity and maybe they will hire you later on. I don't play that game. If I'm delivering value to a company's employees through a presentation or other interaction, I'm entitled to be compensated for that value. I've sometimes given a short presentation as a kind of audition, which has indeed led to a more substantive engagement. But I still insist on being paid for the short talk.

On client relations

A client who engages a new consultant is taking a risk. What if she doesn't have as much experience or knowledge as she claims and doesn't offer good advice? What if a trainer is not a good presenter and the students don't find the class interesting or useful?

Shortly before I went out on my own, I brought a well-known consultant and author into Kodak to teach a one-day class. He was highly entertaining but provided little useful content, stimulated no class discussion, incorporated not a single exercise into the presentation, and provided no pointers to reference materials for more information. The class evaluations were mediocre, and I felt a little stupid. We never brought him back.

I don't want to be a consultant like that or to have my clients telling stories about me like this one. To help my clients reach a comfort level with hiring me, I always

Provide a money-back guarantee.

My goal is for every client to feel that they would happily work with me again. Fortunately, no client has ever asked for a refund, but I'm fully prepared to reduce the fee if they don't feel they got their money's worth.

Periodically I receive emails or phone calls from people who have read one of my books or heard a presentation and want some advice about their situation. I'm always happy to

Answer the first question for free.

Sometimes this reply leads to an ongoing dialogue, but of course it's not feasible for anyone to provide unlimited free consulting to everyone who writes to them. Therefore, if the person who contacted me has more questions, I will offer him an off-site consulting agreement so we can continue the discussion at my usual hourly consulting rate. That offer generally terminates the discussion, although occasionally it leads to an interesting short-term consulting engagement.

I do always provide a substantive response to the initial question, so I'm frankly surprised at how seldom the questioners even acknowledge receipt of my reply or say thank you. That seems kind of rude.

So there you have some of the policies I've adopted during my twenty-three years as a consultant and trainer. It's worth thinking about your own business policies, writing them down if necessary, adjusting them in the face of reality and experience, and applying them consistently. Except when it makes more sense to do something different, of course.

Chapter 18

For Your Protection

(with Gary K. Evans)

As an independent consultant, you must provide for yourself and your family the health, life, and disability insurance that regular employees get from their employers. You must also obtain coverage to protect your business practice. Insurance is a significant expense, but it's mandatory—you're conducting a business, not playing a game of chance. Coverage and exclusions vary widely, so shop around and carefully compare the coverages each type of policy provides.

You're tempting fate and gambling with your home, livelihood, and future if you don't consider at least the six types of insurance described in this chapter. Remember, nothing in this book constitutes legal advice. Check with your lawyer and insurance agent to understand your coverage needs.

Business liability

This coverage affords protection against liability if you cause harm or damage while engaged in business activities. You should never even consider walking onto a client's location if you do not have liability coverage. If you hit a client's employee with your car in the parking lot, or if you trip over a power cord and send a workstation crashing to the floor, you'll want some financial protection. Your personal automotive or umbrella liability insurance might not cover you in such a case. Even if it provides coverage, the limits might not be adequate to protect your business. Consider coverage of at least $1 million per incident, with $2 million general aggregate coverage.

Business property

As you'd expect from the name, this type of policy covers losses you might suffer to your business property, such as electrical damage, a dropped laptop, theft, and so on. If you operate your business from your home, your homeowner's insurance policy may or may not provide coverage if equipment or materials that you use in your business are destroyed, say, in a fire.

I (Karl) obtain my business liability and business property coverage from the same company where I also have my automobile, homeowner's, and other personal insurance policies. Depending on what coverage limits and deductibles you have for business liability and property insurance, the premiums should be in the range of three hundred dollars per year.

I did have to file a claim under my business property policy once. My laptop experienced a static discharge that killed the mouse buttons. It couldn't be repaired. My insurance agent told me to buy a new computer and send him the bill. They immediately reimbursed me for the cost of the replacement computer, less my deductible of one hundred dollars. That one incident made up for several years of the premiums I paid for this coverage.

Professional liability

Also called professional indemnity, errors and omissions, and E&O insurance, this is malpractice insurance against liability caused by negligence or a mistake on your part that causes financial loss or bodily harm to a client or a client's customer. This is for civil liability, not criminal. Certain types of consulting services are more likely to need E&O coverage than others. You might consider an E&O policy if your business includes designing, developing, testing, or certifying products for your clients. Ask a lawyer about this one.

I (Karl) have never carried E&O insurance. I do not create software or software-containing products that my clients use themselves or sell to their clients. I primarily provide advisory and training services, although for certain clients I have also created process-related documents such as templates for key project deliverables, process descriptions, and the like. To be sure, malpractice could extend to providing bad advice or failing to provide appropriate advice. I think my risk exposure is low here though.

Along with my money-back guarantee, my consulting and training agreements include a limitation of liability clause, which states that I am not responsible if the client experiences any loss or lack of benefit from the services or products I deliver. My intent here is to avoid being sued if the client complains that a class was no good just because, say, the students never applied any of the practices I taught them. So far, no client has ever asked for a refund, and I haven't been sued. I'm keeping my fingers crossed. You might feel more comfortable carrying actual insurance coverage, not just crossing your fingers.

Life

If you're single, make sure you have enough life insurance—or money in the bank—to bury yourself. If you have a family, carry enough to protect them for the years you would have provided for them had you survived. Carrying too little life insurance means your spouse might have to go to work or get a second job to provide replacement income for your children's education or the million other necessities of daily life.

To determine how much you really need, explore available commercial and shareware programs and insurance calculators on the internet. Term life insurance policies are cheapest for younger workers, but a whole-life policy may be more appropriate if you have trouble saving money on your own, as it builds up cash value over time. You can take out a loan against the cash value that a whole-life policy accrues, but not against a term life policy. Talk with a trusted insurance agent to understand the options and tradeoffs.

Health care

Although it's a necessity, concerns about health insurance frighten many people contemplating the move to independence. But it need not be such a scary proposition. As a short-term solution, if you leave your employer, voluntarily or not, you are generally entitled to continue receiving your health insurance coverage through a program called COBRA, the Consolidated Omnibus Budget Reconciliation Act of 1985. You pay the full cost of the premiums that likely were partially subsidized by your employer for up to eighteen months of continued coverage. The benefits office at your company should be able to help you with COBRA coverage. After those eighteen months, you are on your own to find health care insurance.

Prior to passage of the Affordable Care Act, health insurance could be prohibitively expensive or even unavailable if you or your family members had a history of medical problems (pre-existing conditions). As of this writing, the health care insurance market is facing significant turbulence. I encourage you to carefully consider your insurance needs, and explore the offerings from every insurance provider in your state to obtain the best value for your family. Seek out advisers who hold the PAHM® (Professional, Academy for Healthcare Management) certification, indicating they are thoroughly knowledgeable in health insurance.

If you're used to getting your health insurance from a traditional corporate employer, be prepared for sticker shock, particularly if you are—how do we say this—older (like us). Premiums, deductibles, coverages, and out-of-pocket maximums vary widely. If you're self-employed, your health insurance premiums may be tax-deductible. Your accountant will know for sure.

You skip this kind of coverage at your peril. Nasty things can happen even if you're young and healthy, and being a road warrior increases the chance of an accident. While on a job in December 2000, I (Karl) slipped and fell on some ice-covered steps in Dallas, Texas. I tore two of the four rotator cuff muscles in my right shoulder. I'm very dominantly right-handed—my left arm exists mainly for visual symmetry—so this was not a fun injury. My insurance covered the visit to the emergency room that night. I didn't have surgery, but I needed quite a bit of physical therapy after I returned home. Had I not had health insurance, this could have been an even more unpleasant experience.

Consider setting up a health savings account if you have a qualifying high-deductible health insurance policy. The HSA allows you to set aside several thousand tax-deductible dollars per year in a special bank account. You can use this account to pay out-of-pocket medical expenses, such as deductibles, prescriptions, and even over-the-counter medications. Not all policies might qualify.

Navigating the plethora of plans available for healthcare can be confusing. It's almost impossible to compare them apples-to-apples, as there are so many variables. An independent insurance broker can help you choose the most appropriate plan for your situation from among the many possibilities.

Disability income

Everyone knows that carrying life insurance to protect your family when you die is worth considering. However, you have a much higher probability of becoming disabled than of dying in any given year. Statistically speaking, a healthy 35-year-old who works in an office has a greater than 20 percent chance of becoming disabled for three months or longer during his or her working career, per www.disabilitycanhappen.org/chances_disability/disability_stats.asp. The duration of the average disability is eighty-two months. That's a long time to go without income.

Disability income insurance provides you with some income if you become disabled and are unable to work. Shop around with multiple agents and providers, because many insurers no longer offer this type of insurance. The coverage that is available comes in various flavors, specifically short-term and long-term disability. Policies vary in their monthly benefits, waiting (or elimination) period before benefits kick in, how long benefits are paid, and so on. Disability policies obtained through professional organizations or your university alumni association, are likely to be cheaper than buying an individual policy directly from an insurance company, but it might not offer as many options. These things always have trade-offs.

Becoming disabled without having disability insurance means that you'll have no life insurance payoff (you're still alive) and you'll be a cost liability (you need to be fed, bathed, cared for, rehabilitated, and so on). Coverage is based on your current income, so review your coverage yearly as your income changes. Depending on your policy, your disability insurance payments might stop when you reach the age of eligibility for full Social Security retirement benefits—but your disability could remain.

As with all insurance, you hope you never have to cash in, because that means something bad happened. But bad things do happen. Karl has a close friend who was a highly regarded software consultant. At age forty-seven Norm suffered a traumatic brain injury in a car accident while driving home from a consulting gig, thanks to an idiot talking on a cell phone. (Please don't talk on your cell phone or text while driving.)

Now age sixty-six, Norm has not worked since that accident in 1999. He will never work again. Norm said that having private disability income insurance made the difference between him being able to continue living in his house and living under a bridge. But when he turned sixty-five, his private disability insurance payments stopped. After that, all he has to live on are his remaining savings and Social Security payments.

By the way, if you are finding this book useful, please consider making a donation to the Norm Kerth Benefit Fund at http://www.processimpact.com/norm_kerth.html. Every dollar helps. Thanks!

A useful tip

Client contracts may require you to carry certain insurance coverages. These are nearly always negotiable, though; see Chapter 16, "Everything's Negotiable." A fellow consultant once gave Gary some great advice on insurance in general. Whenever a client insisted that he carry some obscure type of insurance, he would request that the client pay for it for the duration of the project. That would be factored into the overall cost structure. It never hurts to ask.

Part 4

Building the Business

Chapter 19

A Kind of Business Plan

When I launched my consulting career I didn't have an explicit business plan. I hadn't set any particular goals for myself, let alone devised a strategy for achieving those goals. I just thought I'd see what happened and how my new career shaped up. I don't necessarily recommend this strategy, although it worked out for me.

Once I got established, I did think carefully about how I wanted my consulting career to evolve. I came up with a sort of rudimentary business objective: earn a nice living while I'm asleep. While that's not a true business *plan*, that objective did force the question of "How are you going to do that?"

As an independent consultant with no employees, every penny of revenue I generated came directly through my own efforts. So the trick was to figure out how to generate as much income as possible with as little effort as possible. That is, to look for sources of passive income. I came up with several techniques for creating ongoing revenue streams after some initial investment of effort.

I found some great ideas about generating passive income from a fine book by Alan Weiss called *Money Talks: How to Make a Million as a Speaker*. I've never made a million dollars in a year, but my investment in that book certainly paid off. Weiss wrote another useful book titled *Million Dollar Consulting: The Professional's Guide to Growing a Practice*. I recommend both of these to both aspiring and seasoned consultants.

Income while you sleep #1: Book royalties

Book royalties are a gift that keeps on giving, with some caveats. First, you need to write the book. This is not trivial. I will talk more about that process in Chapter 30, "You Say You Want to Write a Book?" Second, it has to be a good book. Ideally, it will accrue some positive reviews and people will come to recognize the contribution it makes to the practitioners in your field.

Third, the book should fill an important niche in the literature of your domain. For several of my books, I identified gaps in the software literature and attempted to plug them, with generally good success. It's best if the topic you're writing about doesn't have tons of competitive titles or if you have something innovative and unique to share.

Fourth, people need to know about the book, which generally means going with an established publisher rather than self-publishing. You won't get as much money per copy that way, but you will almost certainly sell more copies. Chapter 31, "Getting Your Book into Print," will give you a lot of information about finding and working with a publisher. And fifth, it works best if you write a book that has a long shelf life, not one that deals with the latest fad in your field or with a technology that will be obsolete in a year or two.

Most technical books don't sell zillions of copies. You're probably not going to be able to live on your royalties. I do know a very few people who make more—sometimes a lot more—than $100,000 a year from software book royalties, although I've never approached that lofty pinnacle. Nonetheless, the royalties add up. Once the book is conceived, planned, outlined, proposed to a publisher, contracted, written, reviewed, edited, proofread, published, and promoted, all you need to do is cash the royalty checks. What could be easier?

Income while you sleep #2: Licensing

Most of my work through Process Impact has involved training. The revenue stream from delivering training by yourself is linear: if you teach two classes, you make twice as much money as if you teach one class. To increase the income-to-effort ratio you must disrupt this linear relationship.

One option is to hire other people to teach classes for you and split the revenue. This lets you stay home while someone else wrestles with airplanes, hotels, rental cars, weather, and students. However, having employees or subcontractors complicates your accounting and taxes, at the very least.

I tried a different approach. For many years I have licensed my courseware to other companies. Some of my licensees teach the courses internally to their own staff. Others deliver classes to their own clients or through public seminars. Licensing has worked out well for me.

Obviously, you must first have content available that others find valuable. The content must be structured and packaged such that other people can easily learn to present it effectively. Whenever I developed a new course for my own use, I created detailed instructor notes and supporting information as I went along, with the intent of licensing the material to others.

Some people who license their courseware tell the licensee to let them know when they will be teaching a class. The licensor will then send the requisite number of copies of the student handout to the client site. To me, this suggests that the creator of the materials believes that this is the One True Course on that topic, and that it must always be presented the same way.

I don't take that approach. My licensing agreements give the licensee the right to modify, extend, and subset the licensed material to best meet the needs of each audience. I do this with my own clients; it would be unreasonable not to permit my licensees to do the same for theirs. I described the licensing agreements I use in Chapter 15, "Get It In Writing."

Using this model, after executing the licensing agreement, I'm not involved with how each licensee uses the courseware. I often point prospective clients to two or three of my licensees so the client can consider alternatives to having me teach the class personally. I don't know how much my licensees charge, and I don't care. At the end of every calendar quarter I send an email to each licensee to ask if they delivered any courses. If they did, I get the particulars about duration and number of students, and then I send the licensee an invoice.

Could a licensee lie to me and tell me they only taught three courses when in fact they taught eighty-seven that quarter? Sure. I'd never know. There's a certain amount of trust involved with a licensing arrangement like this. I'm thoughtful about who I'll license the courseware to, as I consider it to be valuable intellectual property. Some of my licensees never teach a course. Others teach dozens. On average, all of us have benefited from the arrangement, as have thousands of students who I could not have reached personally.

I've also licensed various other items for people to incorporate into their own products, courseware, and publications. These materials include white papers or articles I wrote, project document templates I developed, figures or tables from my books, slides to accompany one of my books when it's used as a college text, and the like. I typically charge nominal fees for such licensing.

Just this week, I made $100 by licensing three pages of content to a training company. The total effort involved on my part consisted of a brief email exchange and a faxed licensing agreement. Okay, I wasn't asleep when we worked that out, but the effort was minimal.

Income while you sleep #3: E-learning courseware

After the attacks of 9/11, it occurred to me that people might be more reluctant to travel for training. Therefore, I began exploring ways to package some of my presentations in a CD- or web-based format so people could take my classes from the convenience of their own chairs. After experimenting with different approaches, I settled on an e-learning format that closely mimics my live presentations. There are various ways you can approach e-learning, but this felt right for me because people seem to enjoy my live classes and conference presentations. You can see descriptions and previews of my current suite of e-learning courses at ProcessImpact.com. I also created on-demand webinar versions of several short conference presentations in this same e-learning format.

Over the years, I've sold hundreds of both single-user and corporate-wide site license versions of my e-learning courses. Creating the courses in the first place is a lot of work. I had to learn how to do all that. Preparing slides, creating scripts, recording and cleaning up the audio tracks, synchronizing slide animations with the audio, publishing the whole as a deliverable course, and testing it takes considerable time. Plus, I grew very tired of hearing my own voice drone on hour after hour. But after making that initial investment, the delivery cost and effort is minimal and the profit margin is impressively high.

The e-learning courses also make great train-the-trainer aids for people who license my corresponding instructor-led courseware. I offer my licensees a 50 percent discount on the corresponding e-learning course.

Income while you sleep #4: E-books

Some years ago I wrote several handbooks of approximately seventy pages in length on various topics. Today these would be called e-books. I have sold them as PDF downloads through my website, ProcessImpact.com, both as single-user copies and as site licenses that allow a company to distribute the handbooks throughout their organization. These e-books are inexpensive, but they collectively constitute another small revenue stream that requires negligible effort on my part following the initial investment.

There are numerous web services that handle purchases of these sorts of downloadable products by customers so the purchasing process is entirely automated from your point of view. They manage the shopping cart, the download process, discount codes, and so forth. I use e-Junkie, which has worked fine for me.

It is now quite easy to publish these sorts of e-books through online retailers like Kindle Direct Publishing, Smashwords, IngramSpark, and many others. You can create versions for use with various e-book readers, such as Kindle, NOOK, and Kobo. Chapter 32, "Being Your Own Publisher," describes some of my experiences with self-publishing.

Income while you sleep #5: Other products

I've developed and sold a variety of other products over the years through my website. None of them have generated massive revenue, but it didn't take a great deal of work to create them, and the dollars continue to trickle in. I've retired some that no longer were selling and weren't worth keeping alive. Some products never caught on, but others have yielded considerable income over the years.

The most popular product by far has been the Process Impact Goodies Collection. This is a set of more than sixty document templates, spreadsheet tools, sample project deliverables, e-books, webinars, checklists, and other useful items for requirements development, project management, and peer reviews. Customers can buy small groups of these items in individual sets or they can purchase the entire collection in a single big zip file. Actually, it was a customer who suggested I package all of my downloads into a convenient and low-priced collection like this in 2006. Thanks for the excellent idea, mystery customer!

Best of all, the profits from these downloads go to a consultant who has been disabled with a traumatic brain injury caused by a motor vehicle accident in 1999.

Income while you sleep #6: Affiliate programs

Another way to get free money is to sign up for affiliate or reseller programs. When visitors to your website click through certain links to a vendor's site and buy products there, you get some percentage as a commission. I've been a member of the Amazon Associates program for many years. If you want to see how it works, follow this link, http://amzn.to/2flYVAZ, to the Amazon.com page for my forensic mystery novel, *The Reconstruction*.

Even if you don't buy the book (what?!), once you've clicked in through a link like that you may then browse around Amazon to your heart's content and buy lots of other stuff. I will receive a certain percentage of whatever you spend, and it costs you nothing. Go ahead, try it. Buy many things. Feel free. Do it again later on. Tell your friends about it. I'll let you know how well it works.

Affiliate programs can work the other way, also. I have enlisted several companies to resell my e-learning courses, for instance. When one of their customers buys a course, we split the revenue. Everybody wins. Of course, not all affiliate programs yield actual profits, but once set up, they provide one more way to make money while you sleep.

Is this a great business plan, or what?

Chapter 20

Be Prepared for the Unexpected

Contributed by Claudia Dencker

> *Claudia Dencker is a software business executive with over twenty-five years of team, project, and business management experience in the IT/software service sector. She is currently employed at Stanford University as Director of Special Projects, Business Analysis, and Communications. She is a long-standing member of ASQ and IEEE.*

My career has taken many twists and turns and has been filled with amazing opportunities and successes, as well as its share of disappointments. While I am now an employee of Stanford University, I spent the bulk of my career as an independent consultant. And there is truly no better career.

Many authors have written about the business of consulting, such as how to set yourself up legally, financially, and with the tax authorities. But that's the easy part, because you are in control. You take action, you get results. Where many consultants, business people, and even job candidates fail is in securing the gig, closing the sale, landing the job. Without a stream of consulting assignments, you won't be able to establish or maintain your status as an independent consultant.

This chapter takes you through what I believe are the most important aspects of consulting: establishing a relationship with a client and maintaining that relationship, thereby securing repeat business. Many of these lessons can also be applied to interviewing for a job for regular employment.

I have a nontechnical background. But, I was fortunate enough to be in the right place at the right time when the economy was expanding. I left Hewlett-Packard in 1983 as a software quality engineer with little prospect for advancement unless I got an MBA. The job offer I received from a small start-up in Santa Clara, California, was a compelling step toward realizing the long-held dream of running my own business. This company, a contract software testing house, taught me the necessary skills to take my first step into consulting. I learned the great importance of salesmanship from two masters, one a long-standing salesman and the other a recent graduate from San Jose State University who came to sales naturally.

Before I tell you just what I learned, let me relate a story. Years later, well into my independent consulting career, I was trying to secure some business with a medical device company in San Jose, California. I had already made contact with the decision maker. As part of his qualification process, he wanted me to meet some of the key team members before he made a commitment. I agreed, and we set a date.

On the day of the appointment, thinking that I would only be meeting with two or three people, I drove to the site. It was a stunning day with bright sunshine, blue sky, and a cool breeze blowing through the South Bay, a good omen for the day. As usual, I dressed in business attire and took along some company brochures and business cards in my briefcase, confident that I had a solid chance of landing the job after meeting with a few people.

Imagine my surprise when I entered the conference room and saw twenty people sitting around a large table all waiting to meet me. I took a deep breath, smiled at everyone, and relaxed. This would not be a typical session.

The people around the table introduced themselves. Then came the first question: "Tell us about your services." For those of you interviewing for a job, this is the same question as "Tell us a little about yourself."

I had practiced my pitch many times before in similar settings, in written materials, and through presentations, so I launched into a description of my services. This took about five minutes, as I had pared it to the essentials. I didn't want to talk too much about myself. I wanted to learn from the potential customers what they were looking for, what their pain points were, and how I could help. Only two or three attendees asked questions; everyone else sat and listened. I kept my answers short and to the point, being sure to answer only the question that was asked and nothing more. I even let the occasional silence set in.

Toward the end of the meeting, someone asked another common question: "How much is it going to cost?"

I responded with my usual answer: "Let me review your specifications, and I'll put together a cost for you quickly." I had learned years earlier to avoid giving off-the-cuff estimates. The goal of my meeting with the twenty participants was to get to the next step in the sales cycle. Off-the-cuff cost estimates can slam doors or paint you into corners.

The meeting ended when I had gathered all the information I needed to finalize and price the proposal and to be confident of its success. I had spent much of the meeting listening to the customer, not rushing my answers, and, when I did speak, keeping my answers on point. I tried to keep the customer talking as much as possible.

As I left, I informed everyone that I was very interested. "I want your business," I said. "It would be pleasure to work with you and your team." I'm happy to say that I landed the job. To this day, I still don't know why there were twenty people in the room, as I worked with only one of them.

So what had I learned from the two sales masters that helped me land this contract? Here are the primary lessons:

- Listen, listen, listen. Have the customers tell you what their pain points are; don't assume that you already know. Keep the customers talking and elaborating on their situation. This will help you to form an airtight response to their needs.

- Only answer the question that was asked. Do not elaborate or expand unnecessarily.
- Be prepared for the unexpected (like a much larger interviewing group than you expected).
- Avoid ballparking the cost of your services off the top of your head. Even cost ranges can be booby traps unless they are ridiculously wide, and then everyone will recognize that. This will work against you.
- Be sure to tell the customer that you want their business. In an unexpected way, it is flattering to the customer and, of course, important to you. Your career as an independent consultant starts with that first sale.

Just as importantly, I also learned to relax in those face-to-face meetings. They can be fun.

Chapter 21

How to Get Repeat Business from Your Clients

Contributed by Adriana Beal

Born and raised in Brazil, Adriana Beal (adrianabeal.com) has been working in the U.S. since 2004, helping Fortune 100 companies, innovation companies, and startups build better software that solves the right problem and aligns with business strategy. She has two IT strategy books published in her native country and work published internationally by IEEE and IGI Global. Her educational background includes a B.Sc. in electronic engineering and an MBA in strategic management of information systems.

Any consultant, whether working independently or as part of a consultancy firm, knows that getting repeat business from existing clients is at least as important as finding new clients. When I started providing consulting services to a variety of clients in different industries, I realized that I could classify my clients into two groups:

- Organizations that needed my help for a specific reason that is unlikely to repeat for a long time (for example, a pension fund that no longer needed my services after implementing my recommendations from a fraud risk assessment)

- Organizations that could benefit from my services from time to time, if they liked the results of the work I performed (the majority of my clients)

Obviously, I provided the same level of dedication to clients that were unlikely to need my services again as to firms that I knew could offer me repeat business. However, based on this classification, I was able to adopt metrics to monitor my performance as a consultant. I estimated that two years was enough time for another complex software project—the type of work I specialize in—to surface in a typical organization. Therefore, one indicator of my performance was the percentage of companies from the second group that offered me repeat business within a two-year period.

Recently, I realized that of more than ten consulting clients I have had since moving to the United States in 2004, only one had not yet asked me for repeat business. Even this exception didn't reflect dissatisfaction with my services, as a couple of executives kept in touch with me after the work ended, and one of them hired me to consult for his new employer when he changed jobs. Therefore, I thought I'd be a good candidate to answer a question Karl Wiegers posed: If you get repeat business over the years from the same clients, why do they keep calling you?

Combining my own observations with testimonials from former clients, here are the top three reasons why I believe the same companies kept calling me back during the past decade. I suspect these practices would also help you retain your clients.

Applying systems thinking skills

Systems thinking is a way of understanding reality that emphasizes the relationships among a system's parts, rather than the parts themselves. This is one of the most valuable skills for a consultant. Systems thinking doesn't apply just to information systems, but rather to any system (people, organizations, and so on) whose components are interconnected in such a way that they produce their own pattern of behavior over time.

It's difficult to provide an example of how systems thinking can improve project results without talking extensively about the characteristics of a particular system. To illustrate my point, I'll use a simple case. One of my e-commerce projects received a change request to add a screening process during checkout to prevent certain products from being sold in regions where their sale was restricted by law. The business stakeholders approved the requirements, and the team was ready to start coding the solution.

However, I realized that what seemed to be a simple change affecting only one step during the checkout process also affected other business areas, including the call center operation. Without other changes, such as a new feature in the call center application to allow agents to filter out restricted items when recommending products to a customer, the sales process would suffer. Call center representatives would run the risk of wasting time convincing a customer to buy a product, only to learn at checkout time that the product could not be ordered from that location. This would increase the risk of customer frustration, lead to a higher abandon rate, and increase the handle time of inbound calls.

Systems thinkers aim to enhance total system properties, rather than trying to optimize certain parts of the system. A good resource is *Thinking in Systems: A Primer* by the late scientist Donella Meadows. Meadows explains such phenomena as why everyone in a system can act dutifully and rationally and yet still have those well-meaning actions add up to a terrible result, and why a system might suddenly and without warning jump into a completely unexpected behavior.

By using systems thinking, you will be able to forge more creative and satisfactory solutions for your clients, ensuring that separate groups keep the whole in mind while working on their individual parts. When a new challenge arises, the client will remember the benefit of bringing in an external consultant who is mindful of such causal relationships.

Being truthful and straightforward

I've always been very candid with my clients, telling them when I thought an idea didn't sound feasible or a solution didn't seem effective. Often, a team member would disagree with my approach, but throughout the years I kept my belief that speaking up early and honestly about problems improves your results and increases client satisfaction.

Here's an example, based on a common business problem. In one of my client companies, the IT group had not met a software release date in years and budgets were out of control. As part of the process improvement initiative I was leading, the head of development wanted his project teams to stop lying and hiding problems that threatened the completion date, something they did mostly to look good in meetings. This manager's proposed approach was to confront his subordinates and demand a change in behavior.

The problem, however, was that "lying to look good" was a practice that permeated even the top management layer. The only way to solve the problem was to acknowledge the role executives and managers played in it. It wasn't easy to discuss this sensitive issue with my client, but being honest about the need for change to come from the top allowed us to modify the signals the development teams received from senior management.

Before this problem was addressed, team members would hide issues they were experiencing, opting instead to wait until another person reported a delay. Their hope was to get the extra time they needed without having to be identified as the "source" of the project slippage. With the change in behavior starting from the top, the teams became more comfortable speaking up and dealing with any problem that threatened project success as soon as possible. Such change caused a significant decrease in delivery delays, defects, and runaway costs.

During project retrospectives, clients who later went on to hire me again frequently provided positive feedback related to my ability to speak up early and honestly about project issues. This "culture of candor" was seen by these clients as an essential early-warning system to eliminate or minimize project risks in a timely manner.

Putting your client's interests before yours

As a consultant, sometimes I saw that I was not the right person to take on an assignment or that the project I was being hired to assist did not have a solid business case. Even though taking the assignment would be financially desirable for me in the short term, my client always appreciated my addressing such concerns directly with them. In several cases, the client and I were able to rethink the project's mission and purpose, if necessary canceling either the initiative or my involvement in it. Whenever this type of situation arose over the last ten years, it led to repeat business with that client or referrals to other companies that could use my services.

By being candid with your clients, even when the truth is not in your best short-term interest, you help paint a picture of the real problems. You also reassure the clients that you will stay with your mission and purpose and not compromise your principles. Most clients will appreciate your transparency. It opens an opportunity for you to build solid relationships with those with whom you're doing working.

Getting repeat business from your clients, as well as referrals from them, is one of the most effective ways of growing a consulting business. My approach is not the only successful strategy to achieve this goal, but the practices described here have helped me develop lasting and profitable relationships with my consulting clients. However, as with everything else in life, there is no one-size-fits-all solution. Each consultant needs to find a system that works well for her.

Chapter 22

Participating in Professional Organizations

Perhaps it's because I began my career as a research scientist, but I've always thought it was important to join and participate in the activities of professional societies. Over the years I have been a member of the American Chemical Society, Association for Computing Machinery, Institute of Electrical and Electronics Engineers (IEEE), IEEE Computer Society, American Society for Quality, and others. Participating in such organizations helps promote professionalism and distribute knowledge among the members. Society meetings and conferences provide many opportunities for networking, which can lead to employment possibilities both for independent consultants and for those seeking regular jobs. You can also make new friends.

Since I became an author and speaker in the software arena, I have received many invitations to speak at local, national, and international meetings of various professional organizations. One came in just today, in fact. These organizations have included the International Institute of Business Analysis (IIBA), Project Management Institute (PMI), IEEE, and various software process improvement networks (SPINs) around the country.

Speaking at organizations like these, particularly at local meetings, is a great way to try out new material. I can practice a new keynote presentation in a friendly environment before I have to deliver it to hundreds of people at a big conference. I've also delivered webinars for such organizations from the comfort of my home office, thereby extending my visibility and impact beyond those who could attend a particular conference or meeting.

I view these presentations both as a way to contribute to my technical community and as a marketing tool. Earlier in my career, presentations at local professional organization meetings did generate quite a few training and consulting opportunities, although that is no longer true. When we can work out the logistics, I'm always happy to make those kinds of presentations.

I don't charge a fee to speak at local professional organization meetings. Some people seem puzzled when I explain that it's not feasible for me to fly across the country—let alone across an ocean—to give a short talk and then fly home again, without compensation, even if they reimburse my travel expenses. The argument that "it will be great visibility for you and might lead to some work" is not persuasive.

When travel is involved, I try to arrange these presentations to piggyback on some work I'm already doing in the vicinity. Sometimes, the professional group has contacts with a local training company that can arrange for me to deliver a public, open-enrollment seminar. This generates some revenue for me so I can stay an extra day to speak at the professional group meeting. Because I'm not being paid for that presentation, I'm not shy about promoting my books, e-learning courses, and other products and services. Maybe some attendees will buy one of my books afterward and tell their friends about it. I might give the attendees a secret discount code for, say, 30 percent off the Process Impact Goodies Collection.

Numerous organizations have established professional certification programs for people working in information technology. Among many others, these include:

- Certified Business Analysis Professional (CBAP) and others from IIBA
- Certified Professional for Requirements Engineering (CPRE) from the International Requirements Engineering Board (IREB)
- Project Management Professional (PMP), PMI Agile Certified Practitioner (PMI-ACP), and PMI Professional

in Business Analysis (PMI-PBA) from PMI
- Certified Software Quality Engineer (CSQE) from ASQ

If you work in some field other than IT, you doubtless have your own suite of professional organizations and certifications to consider.

These professional certifications typically are earned through a combination of education, work experience, and passing an examination based on a body of knowledge established for the discipline. Whole industries have grown up to provide exam-preparation training. I fear this sometimes results in "teaching to the test" as opposed to necessarily helping the candidate acquire the right set of practical knowledge and skills to enhance her job performance. Ideally, these objectives are congruent, but I'm not sure that is always the case.

You might consider whether having one or more of these abbreviations following your name would enhance your professional credentials and make you more attractive to prospective clients or employers. I've always had great respect for adults who went back to school or committed to focused self-study to obtain advanced degrees or professional certifications. This shows a serious commitment to continuous learning and growth of one's knowledge, skills, and capabilities.

I don't hold any certifications myself. The only letters I can put after my name are "MS" and "PhD" and those were in organic chemistry. Some people seem to collect certifications, appending a long string of abbreviations to their name. Following are some of the most extreme examples I've seen:

- ACS, ALMI, CSM, FIII, IPGDRM, MIB, AHM, SAFe
- PMI-ACP, PMP, SPS, PSM, PSPO, MCP
- MBA, PMP, RMP, SIPM, PRINCE2, CABA, CAT
- MSc, PhD, PMP, CSM, CSP, PMI-ACP
- PMP, MIET, MQSi, MCIOB, MRICS
- PMI (PBA, ACP), PROSCI, ITILv3, PSM, PSPO

I have no idea what most of those abbreviations stand for. It looks impressive—and maybe it really is—but spending significant time studying to get certified isn't necessarily as valuable as gaining a lot of practical, hands-on experience. I wonder if the objective for some of those collectors is merely procurement of the credential, not the effective application of all that hard-learned knowledge. Do you think anyone would notice if I were to recast my professional identity as Karl Wiegers, MS, PhD, MIC, KEY, MO-USE?

If you are—or hope to become—an independent consultant, I encourage you to join relevant professional organizations and participate in their local activities. I enjoy meeting the people who attend these sessions. Sometimes there's pizza or cookies. In some cases I've established contacts and relationships that have persisted for years. The networking opportunities might indeed help you generate some visibility and possibly some consulting leads.

If you are already established in your field, then appearing at such events is a goodwill gesture that helps enhance your reputation as a constructive contributor to the community and all-around nice person. That's not a bad image to cultivate.

Part 5

Media Matters

Chapter 23

Out of One, Many

When I began speaking at software conferences, I wondered if I needed to develop a new presentation each time I spoke. Some other speakers I knew thought this was necessary. I quickly learned that it was not. In fact, I have delivered certain short presentations more than two dozen times in various forums: conferences, professional society meetings, webinars, and client sites. Generalizing this insight, you should try to leverage the intellectual property (IP) you create as an independent consultant as many ways as you can. Let me give you a great example.

In 1999 a magazine editor invited me to write a short article, just fifteen hundred words, with "twenty or thirty quick project management tips" to plug a hole in their editorial calendar. In about ninety minutes I banged out a piece titled "Secrets of Successful Project Management." Over the years I have built on this small starting point in numerous ways.

- By adding some more content, I created a one-hour presentation called "21 Project Management Success Tips," which I've delivered twelve times. The written version of the material—an enhanced version of the original short article—appeared in the proceedings of numerous conferences.
- I created an on-demand webinar version of "21 Project Management Success Tips."
- The enhanced "21 Project Management Success Tips"

paper was incorporated in a compilation of software project management articles published by the IEEE Computer Society.
- By adding another dozen topics, drilling down into more detail on them, and building in several practice activities, I expanded the one-hour talk into a full-day course called "Project Management Best Practices." I've taught this course twenty times at companies, government agencies, and conferences.
- I created an e-learning version of the "Project Management Best Practices" course.
- I selected about three dozen slides from the "Project Management Best Practices" e-learning course and packaged them as the "5-Minute Manager" e-learning series, with quick-hitting micro-tutorials on focused topics for busy people who don't need to take a whole course.
- I wrote a series of articles amplifying some of the project management tips, which were published in various print and online magazines.
- I collected several of these papers into my "Project Initiation Handbook."
- I combined the contents of the "Project Initiation Handbook" with several other articles I wrote on project management and some new material and published the result as a book titled *Practical Project Initiation: A Handbook with Tools*.
- Going the other direction, I serialized selected chapters from *Practical Project Initiation* and republished them as articles on a project management-oriented website.

The moral of the story is this: as you create your own intellectual property, look for opportunities to leverage it into other forms, both to increase your visibility and to generate revenue. An article can turn into a podcast or a video, and vice versa. People learn in different ways, so packaging high-quality content for delivery in various media and through multiple channels increases its potential value to your audiences.

Do the rights thing

If you publish an original article in a magazine or on a website, make sure your contract gives you the right to reuse the material in a future book and to license it to other channels for reprinting. That is, you want to give the magazine "first serial rights" to the piece. The key word in the contract is "nonexclusive," meaning that you're not restricted from using the material elsewhere. You might need to acknowledge the original publisher when you reprint materials and indicate that it is being reprinted with permission from that publisher.

Some publishers want only original material. Therefore, if you submit previously published material to another source, make sure to state that it has appeared previously so they can decide if it's right for them. I ask a lower fee for previously-published material than I do for a new article.

If you publish a book with a traditional publisher, be sure the contract gives you the right to repurpose content adapted from the book into other forms, such as magazine articles and blog posts. I have licensed many such derived articles to multiple websites, each of which generates a small amount of money. Starting the other way, if you write a series of blog posts you might be able to combine them into e-books and perhaps ultimately into a full book. You know, like this one.

Who owns it?

You have to be careful how you use materials that you write or create exclusively for a single client at their request. You do not own the rights to such a work for hire—the client does. Therefore, you may not normally reuse or resell that material without permission.

On a few occasions, I have negotiated with a client to retain the right to reuse material I created for them, usually by cutting my fee in half, so that we have joint ownership. These sorts of negotiations are perfectly fine, if the client doesn't mind. I recommend you get a statement of any such agreement in writing to protect yourself in the future.

The same holds true if you create presentations or write articles while you're a regular employee of another company. Make sure you clarify who owns the material. I had to do this when I was writing for publication while I worked at Kodak. I made sure that I did all my writing on my own time and my own computer. All of the materials I created for presentation or publication went through Kodak's corporate clearance process; I had the thickest corporate clearance folder at the company. When I left Kodak, I asked my manager to write a letter explicitly acknowledging my ownership of specified materials I had created during my tenure there. It's best to avoid any possible confusion and legal entanglements.

By the way, delivering your intellectual property to diverse customers in a variety of forms is a tip I picked up from Alan Weiss's very useful books *Money Talks: How to Make a Million as a Speaker* and *Million Dollar Consulting: The Professional's Guide to Growing a Practice*. Those books were worth every penny I paid for them.

Chapter 24

On Intellectual Property

As a consultant, speaker, and writer, you will be creating valuable intellectual property. You must protect that intellectual property, because it's how you earn your living. The flip side is to make sure that you properly respect other people's intellectual property.

Most people I know are sensible, honest, and fair when it comes to these matters. Sadly, a few are not. In this chapter I address certain aspects of copyright, intellectual property rights, and courtesies. Let me reiterate that nothing I say here constitutes legal advice. Also, intellectual property laws vary from country to country.

Copyright notices

Contrary to popular belief, you do not need to officially register your copyright on something you created with the United States Copyright Office to protect it. The act of creating the item automatically grants copyright ownership to the creator. However, placing a copyright notice on the item provides you with certain legal benefits.

According to the U.S. Copyright Office, a properly composed copyright notice consists of the following three elements:

1. The copyright symbol, ©; the word "copyright;" or the abbreviation "copr.," but not "(c)"
2. The year of first publication of the work, or the year of creation if the work is unpublished
3. The name of the copyright owner

You might also wish to include a statement of the rights you are reserving. My copyright notices generally look like this:

Copyright © 2018 Karl Wiegers. All rights reserved.

Sometimes I create items, such as document templates, that I intend for people to use as the starting point for their own project deliverables. I place a copyright notice like the following on such document templates:

Copyright © 2018 Karl Wiegers. Permission is granted to use and modify this document.

I want to make it clear that people may use this document and modify it to best suit their needs, but that I own the copyright on the template itself. They may not claim it as their own IP, sell it to their own clients, post it on public websites (which, alas, happens all the time), or anything like that. Of course, I make no ownership claims on any documents a project team creates from my templates.

Although I do not register copyrights with the U.S. Copyright Office for most of the items I create, I certainly do for my books. A commercial publisher takes care of that as part of the publication process. For books that I self-publish, it's my responsibility to register the copyright. That process consists of filling out the appropriate form from the U.S. Copyright Office (https://www.copyright.gov), paying a modest fee, and sending them two copies of the book. For more information, see the publication "Copyright Basics" at https://www.copyright.gov/circs/circ01.pdf.

Citing the work of others

When I was a graduate student in organic chemistry, I read a lot of journal articles and wrote a few myself. I learned the importance of crediting other sources on which I relied in the books and articles I write now. Citing other publications and their authors accomplishes two objectives. First, it gives credit to those who have done previous work in the area. With but rare exceptions, we all build on the work of others. I incorporate what I learn from them into my own thinking and creations; therefore, I should acknowledge their contributions. And second, citing other sources gives the interested reader places to go for more information or supporting evidence for my positions.

I look askance at technical publications that contain no references. It's unusual for an individual to invent a whole new domain of study entirely on his own. Omitting references implies that the author is claiming credit for all of the material presented in his publication.

If you have some sources that you want to cite in an article, learn how the periodical to which you are submitting it handles citations. Format your references in the same way you see done in other articles in the periodical. Books typically list references at the end, sequenced alphabetically by author, although sometimes each chapter will list the sources cited therein at the end. A bibliography of sources for further reading on certain topics isn't the same thing as a list of the references you cited at specific points in your text. Both have their place.

Be sure to check your citations scrupulously for completeness and accuracy. I've seen many erroneous references to my own publications: incorrect first name or middle initial, last name misspelled, incomplete or inaccurate title, incorrect publication date, and the like. I'm embarrassed to confess that I've made a few of those same kinds of mistakes myself. No matter how carefully you check them, it's easy to have an error slip into a reference citation.

Fair use

Occasionally you might wish to incorporate material created by someone else into your own work. Of course, the first thing you have to do is to cite the original source. If you don't own the copyright to a work, then you might also need to get permission from the copyright owner to reuse their material. The exception is if the amount and type of material that you wish to use lies within the domain of "fair use." The U.S. Copyright Office comments on fair use at https://www.copyright.gov/fair-use/more-info.html.

Remember, a copyright notice does not have to appear on the material for it to be considered copyrighted. If you created some intellectual property—a book, article, poem, or song—you own the copyright to it unless you've granted that copyright to some other party. For instance, with a work made for hire, the employer is considered the legal owner of the copyright to the work. Your contract with that employer should stipulate ownership of any materials created under the contract. If you don't own the copyright to some IP, please respect the owner's rights.

Unfortunately, what exactly constitutes "fair use" is not well defined. As I understand it, in general it is permissible to include short quotations or excerpts ("short" being undefined) in your own work without explicit permission, provided that you cite the original source. However, if either a significant fraction of your work is derived from someone else's work, or if you are incorporating a significant portion of someone else's work into yours ("significant" being undefined), then you need permission from the copyright owner. If you wish to include a complete table, figure, poem, or the like from someone else's work in your work, request permission.

As document FL102 by the U.S. Copyright Office stated, "The distinction between fair use and infringement may be unclear and not easily defined. There is no specific number of words, lines, or [musical] notes that may safely be taken without permission. *Acknowledging the source of the copyrighted material does not substitute for obtaining permission* [emphasis mine]."

I recently read an online article, adapted from a forthcoming book, that centered on a large table of information. That table was clearly based on a similar table from one of my own books. The author had added some value, but more than half of the material he presented was in fact *my* material, nearly verbatim. The author did not even include a citation to my original publication. I felt this went well beyond fair use, as he had essentially incorporated my entire table into his work, with neither acknowledgment nor permission.

I contacted the author, who replied that he planned to list my book in his book's general bibliography of resources. I didn't think that was adequate. I explained that a specific citation to my original source when he presented his table was necessary; requesting permission in advance was even better. The author balked but did check with his publisher, who wisely agreed with me. Citing another author's work costs you nothing; just do it.

Licensing fees

It's within the rights of the copyright owner to request a licensing fee for you to reuse their material. For instance, I paid a licensing fee to include a Dilbert comic in one of my books. The comic was a perfect fit, well worth the modest cost.

Periodically I receive requests from people to include content from my books, articles, or websites in something they are creating. Sometimes what they're requesting lies within my understanding of fair use and it's no problem. If they wish to use my material for academic purposes or to share small items within their company, I'm generally happy to grant permission. I do try to be reasonable and fair. And I always appreciate people who go to the trouble to ask first.

Other times, though, someone wants to incorporate a figure, a complete document template, or some other resource I've created in a book or training course they'll be using for commercial gain. I generally ask a small licensing fee in these cases. They're going to make money in part from material I created, so I'm entitled to a little nibble of the pie. If that's okay with the person who made the request, we make a deal; other times they decide not to use my material after all. Either way is fine with me.

Protecting your intellectual property

I've had both amusing and dismaying experiences in which people have misappropriated my intellectual property. Let me share some of those experiences so you can be alert for similar problems with your own creations.

I once read an article about a software quality technique called inspection, a type of formal peer review, in a respected software journal. The author was a man of unimpeachable integrity, a titan of the software industry whom I admire greatly. Someone else, whom I didn't know, had written a two-page sidebar to accompany the article that presented an overview of software peer reviews. As I read the sidebar, I found myself agreeing with what it said. Then I realized why: I wrote it!

This sidebar was nothing but a condensation and paraphrasing of an article I had published in a different magazine several years earlier. I'm the only person who ever would have noticed that connection, and I did. However, the author of the sidebar did not cite my article, and she did not have permission from either me or that earlier magazine for this adaptation.

I easily convinced the journal's editor of the similarities between my article and the sidebar. He issued a clarification and apology in the next issue. I also wrote to the author of the sidebar, but she never replied. Had the author contacted me and asked about presenting this summary, with due credit given to the original source, I would have said fine. Instead, she simply took my material, rephrased it somewhat, and presented it as her own. That's not fine.

On another occasion I was sitting with a friend at a conference. The speaker was talking about some aspect of software requirements, a field in which I've done quite a lot of work. He showed a slide and said, "I'm not sure where I found this." My friend grinned at me and whispered, "I think I know."

The slide was pulled right out of one of my training courses. This was flattering, naturally, but it was also curious. I had never taught that course at the speaker's company, so I'm not sure how he got it. After the talk, I told him where that slide came from. He apologized, but I told him he could continue to use it if he added a reference to the source.

Recently I discovered one of my magazine articles posted on three other websites. On one, no author was listed, implying that the website's owner wrote the piece. I called the owner, who agreed to show my name as the author, as he should have done in the first place. On the other two sites, different people showed their own names as the author, even though the article was lifted nearly verbatim from my site. It's highly irritating to have other people claim my work as their own. I work hard on the things I write.

I have long offered various templates and other project aids for downloading from my websites. I once discovered another website that offered a use-case document template for downloading. Their template was identical to the one on my site, except that someone had replaced my copyright notice with her own. You can't do that.

When I pointed this out, the woman I contacted initially claimed she had created her template prior to mine, so therefore *I* was the copyright violator. I then called her attention to the Microsoft Word document properties for her file, where my name was still listed as the document's author! She then reluctantly acknowledged that mine was the original and agreed to take hers down. If you're going to steal something, you'd better do it right.

I keep an eye on how my intellectual property is misused not because of ego, of making sure that I always get full "credit" for anything I've ever said or written. Instead, it's a matter of making sure that the intellectual property from which I earn a living remains my property.

Some years ago I received an email from someone I didn't know, asking if my *Software Requirements* book was now in the public domain. It was not. She had spotted an article that clearly was cribbed from that book, which wasn't referenced. I contacted the author and learned that this was the first in a series of three articles, indeed drawn from my book, without citation or permission.

The author was not an American, although he was living in the United States. He told me that summarizing another author's work like this was considered a compliment in his country. I replied that it was considered plagiarism in the United States. It was too late to withdraw part two of the series from the publication cycle, but we got my name listed as a co-author for part three, along with the reference to my book. I'm not trying to be mean here, but I do have to protect the material that I have created—with a considerable investment of effort—so that the ownership and any revenues ensuing from it remain mine.

Here's another interesting example of misappropriation. Several years ago I discovered a website based in another country that had reposted numerous articles that were originally published in *Software*

Development magazine, including several of mine. One problem was that the people who created this website had not obtained permission from the publisher of *Software Development* nor from the original authors to post these articles. Another problem was that they had moved the original author's name to the fine print at the end of each article, putting someone else's name at the top so it looked like this other person wrote it. I worked with the original magazine's publisher to get that website to halt this unethical practice.

A risk of writing

My sister, who also is an IT professional, once took a class on software requirements at her company. During his presentation, the young instructor referred to something I had written, calling it "the Wiegers method." My sister didn't quite understand the point; she asked if he could expand on it. "Sorry," he said, "that's all I know."

"I'll ask him," my sister replied.

That night she gave me a call and told me what the instructor had quoted from my writing. I had no recollection of ever having said what he had attributed to me. I searched through both of my requirements books and didn't find anything like what he had said. She reported that back to the instructor, and I emailed him as well to follow up. I found the whole episode pretty amusing.

A risk of sharing your thoughts in public is that others may misunderstand, misinterpret, or miscommunicate them. It happens in both positive and negative directions. Sometimes people have accused me of believing something that in fact I do not believe, because that's how they had interpreted something I wrote, after processing it through their own filters and biases. In other cases, I've received credit for some pithy quotation I had duly cited in my writing, but which I had not originated. If you're going to put yourself out there through writing or speaking, get used to this possibility.

Pure theft

Within a few weeks of publication of my most recent software book, *Software Requirements, 3rd Edition*, in 2013, I found dozens of websites that offered free downloads of the e-book version. I've also seen websites and discussion boards where people were offering free copies of my e-books to anybody who requested one. Of course, the author does not receive any royalties for such pirated book downloads.

This is unethical and illegal. It is called "theft," and it is rampant. It's often hard to discover how to contact the managers of those sites and persuade them to remove the items that are being stolen. Some of them hide behind the façade that they are merely providing links to other sites that are actually doing the stealing, so they aren't responsible for any wrongdoing.

Consequently, I will not be writing any new software books. It seems silly to spend hundreds of hours creating a product only to have unscrupulous people steal it. To be sure, not everyone who downloads a free book would have bought it anyway, but industry experts agree that pirated downloads definitely hurt sales.

If you want a book, buy it. Authors work very hard on their creations, and they are entitled to compensation for their efforts, even in a world in which so many people seem to think anything available on the internet should be free.

The funniest case

For many years, I've made numerous document templates, checklists, spreadsheet tools, and other resources available to be downloaded from the Process Impact Goodies web page at http://www.processimpact.com/goodies.shtml. Some years ago I stumbled onto another consultant's site that offered a similar set of downloadable items. Too similar, in fact. The boilerplate text on his page was lifted verbatim from my Goodies page, and about half of the items he had available for downloading also were taken from my page. (Copyscape.com is a website that lets you search for text copied from a website.) He did identify those items as being mine, but he hadn't asked me for permission to use them in this fashion.

When I first contacted the consultant to inquire about this, he ignored me. I tried again. This time he replied but pushed back against my request that he remove my materials from his site. The guy said, "You don't have to be a <rude term> about it." Oh, great, I thought: name-calling escalation. He takes my material without permission and I'm the <rude term>? Ultimately, he apologized for that comment and complied with my request.

The funny part? The name of this dude's company, now long gone, included the word "Maverick," and he had a dictionary definition of maverick at the top of each page on his website: "someone who exhibits great independence in thought and action." Uh-huh.

Chapter 25

Twelve Tips for Becoming a Confident Presenter

I'm not quite sure how it happened, but somewhere along the way I became a public speaker. I never took a speech class or participated in debate in school. I never attended Toastmasters or any other organization that helps you become comfortable speaking before an audience. Nonetheless, I've delivered well over six hundred presentations in the past twenty-five years and enjoyed just about all of them. Somehow, I have become comfortable speaking for anywhere from thirty minutes to four days, to audiences ranging from just a few people up to eight thousand.

Most consultants will be called upon to give a presentation or teach a class from time to time. Speaking in public is one of the most terrifying experiences for most people. That fear even has a name: glossophobia. The anxiety is understandable. Everyone is staring right at you, eagerly awaiting your words of wisdom. You feel exposed and vulnerable. It's one thing to say something foolish in a private conversation; it's quite a different matter to say it to dozens, hundreds, or thousands. The potential for embarrassment is enormous. However, so is the potential for sharing important information that can influence many people in a positive way. Not to mention the potential for making a lot of money.

Just in case you, like so many other people, are nervous about the idea of giving a presentation, in this chapter I share Karl's Tips for Confident Public Speaking. Keeping these ideas in mind will help chase the butterflies from your stomach. Maybe you'll even have fun the next time you're on stage.

Presentation Tip #1: No one knows what you're going to say next. Don't worry if the words that come out of your mouth don't exactly match the way you planned, scripted, or practiced the talk. Just keep going. A presentation is very different from, say, a piano recital of a well-known musical composition, where someone in the audience is sure to notice a B that should have been a C.

Presentation Tip #2: You are in control. You're the one with the podium, the microphone, the projector, the laser pointer. You're the one who can ask the audience if they have any questions. You can terminate the discussion and move on whenever you like. You control the pacing. It's your show.

Presentation Tip #3: You probably know more about your topic than anyone else in the room. Otherwise, one of them would be speaking and you'd be listening. Even if you're not the world's expert on the subject, you're likely to be the local expert for that hour or day.

It can be disconcerting to deliver a presentation at a conference and recognize a well-known authority on the topic in the audience. Most such authorities will keep a low profile and not ask embarrassing questions or try to take over the presentation. At least, that's what I do when I'm attending a talk in my area of expertise. I don't want to make anyone uncomfortable. I might amplify upon an answer to a question if it seems appropriate or if the speaker invites me to. Otherwise, I just sit and listen.

Rarely, I have seen a famous person take an inappropriately intrusive role in someone else's presentation. I find that highly irritating; the speaker probably does as well. So if you're the famous person at someone else's talk, please remember that it's the speaker's show, not yours.

Presentation Tip #4: You rarely face a hostile audience. Most people are there because they want to hear what you have to say. This isn't necessarily true if you're dealing with a controversial issue or if you're speaking at a political or government meeting of some kind. But if you're delivering a factual presentation to a group of people who are attending of their own volition, they usually start out with an open and receptive attitude. After that, it's up to you to hold their interest and persuade them of the merits of your material.

Keynote presentations at conferences might constitute an exception to this tip. A keynote topic sometimes is deliberately provocative, chosen to stimulate the thinking or trigger the emotions of the audience. In a case like that, you should expect a more energetic reaction from the audience than usual.

I opted for this approach the very first time I gave a keynote, at a software process improvement conference with some eighteen hundred attendees back in 1999. In fact, the man who invited me to do the keynote told me to bring my most stimulating and provocative material. So I came up with the title "Read My Lips: No New Models!" My premise was that the software industry already had plenty of models and methods for increasing quality and productivity. What we lacked was the effective and consistent application of those established techniques. So I was encouraging people not to develop any more new models just then, but rather to work on reduction to practice of what we already knew worked.

This was somewhat provocative because the organization that sponsored this large conference had led the development of many of the models about which I was saying "Enough!" When I reached the podium, I was slightly taken aback to see the man who began this whole improvement-model movement sitting in the very front row. I had never met him, although of course I knew his work. He didn't say anything during the presentation (see Presentation Tip #3), but his body language wasn't encouraging.

Years later, I met someone who had sat with that luminary at my presentation. I was relieved to learn that his reaction to my thesis was: "Karl's right." I'm not sure everyone who attended the conference agreed, but my keynote certainly did stimulate discussion that went on for the duration of the event. That was my goal.

Presentation Tip #5: Avoid saying "and on the next slide…" I learned this tip from my thesis advisor in graduate school. Maybe you don't remember just what's on the next slide, or you changed the sequence from the last time you gave the presentation. When we used actual 35mm slides decades ago, they might not have been loaded in the slide carousel exactly as you planned.

If you say "on the next slide" but you're surprised by what then pops up, you might have to backtrack a bit. Awkward. Instead, just display the next slide in the sequence and talk about whatever is on it. In other words, it's okay to fake it a little bit. You have to roll with reality even when it doesn't match the plan.

Presentation Tip #6: Don't read the slides to the audience. They can all read just fine (assuming you've used a suitably large font—consider the room size when laying out your slides). Reveal elements of the slide, such as bullets or graphics, one at a time, instead of showing an entire complex slide and then leading the audience through it.

To prompt your memory, especially with a new presentation, you can use the notes view in PowerPoint to write the abstract of what you want to say about each slide. If you need the reminders during your talk, you can keep a stack of printed notes pages on the table or podium in front of you and unobtrusively flip the pages while you're speaking. If you need more space for text, put sticky notes on the back of the preceding page so they're visible when you flip to the next notes page.

I have presented many webinars, in which I'm speaking from the comfort of my home office over the phone, displaying slides through the internet to attendees all over the world. Because no one can see me during those presentations, I can make the presentation process easy for myself. I write rich notes for each of my slides in a conversational style, based on how I have given the presentation live in the past. That way I can just read the notes, with appropriate vocal inflections and additional commentary relevant to that audience. The PowerPoint notes thus serve as a script, enabling me to give a natural-sounding presentation of repeatably high quality.

Presentation Tip #7: It's okay to say "I don't know" in response to a question. If you aren't sure how best to respond, that's better than standing there silently because you can't think of the right answer. It's also better than making up an answer on the fly that might turn out to be wildly erroneous. Even better than a simple "I don't know" is "I don't know, but I'll find out," or "I'm not sure off the top of my head, so let me think about your question and get back to you." Then make sure you follow up later on.

Because you are controlling the presentation (see Presentation Tip #2), you can also choose to defer questions to the end. You might suggest that you follow up off-line with someone who's asking a complex question or one that's of limited interest to the rest of the audience. And for reasons of time management, you could even decline to answer questions. But do show respect for serious questioners, even if you can't give them all a perfect answer in real time during your presentation slot.

Presentation Tip #8: Watch the clock. Speakers who run past their allotted time get dinged on their evaluations. This goes double if you're speaking just before a break, prior to lunch, or at the end of the day. Try not to run more than one minute past your scheduled finish time.

If you see that you might run out of time before you cover everything you planned to say, that's your problem, not the audience's problem. Skipping some material is much better than holding captive a fidgeting audience who would like to move on with their lives. With practice, you'll get better at selectively condensing your planned material while underway to bring the talk to a smooth close. Nobody likes seeing a speaker Rolodex through twenty slides in the last five minutes.

Similarly, when you're teaching a class, start on time and resume promptly following breaks. I always tell people exactly how long the break will be, and I start right up at the appointed minute. If some people trickle back in late, that's their problem. I've been called a Time Nazi. I took it as a compliment. We have a lot of material to cover, and I don't wish to be constrained by the last person to return to the room.

I plan on spending an average of three minutes discussing each slide. I know one speaker who says he averages just one minute per (information-dense) slide. Particularly toward the end of his overstuffed presentations, he goes so fast that I've given up trying to follow him. While it is good to move along briskly, people can only absorb information at a certain rate. Flashing up a slide for just a few seconds is pointless if the audience gets nothing out of it.

Presentation Tip #9: Be sure to talk about what you said you were going to talk about. I firmly believe in truth in advertising, so I write abstracts for my presentations that are both accurate and inviting. The audience members have a right to know what to expect, and the speaker has a responsibility to deliver. This tip might seem obvious, but I've attended more than one presentation where the content delivered didn't fulfill the promise from the title and the abstract.

Let's say the title is "Conjugating Verbs in Swahili," but the material presented misses the mark. At the end of the talk the speaker invites questions. One attendee asks, "Were you going to say anything about conjugating verbs in Swahili?" The speaker doesn't know how to respond. She thinks that's what she just spent an hour discussing, but she really didn't. That's an embarrassing position for any speaker to be in. I've seen it happen, fortunately not to me.

Presentation Tip #10: Go to the right place. I used to be a regular speaker at a series of software development conferences held in the San Francisco Bay Area. Some years they were at a convention center in San Francisco itself, other times in San Jose or Mountain View. Another regular speaker I knew once went to the San Francisco convention center, but the conference was held in San Jose that year! He had to frantically race the fifty miles to San Jose, barely making it in time for his presentation. It pays to know where you're heading before you make your travel arrangements.

I've been burned by location ambiguity myself a few times. At one client site, I was delivering a two-day course for business analysts followed by a one-day management presentation. Not having been told otherwise, I assumed both presentations would be held in the same location. So on the morning of day three, I went back to the same room where I'd taught the previous two days, only to find a different class going on there. With some effort, I learned that the second class was scheduled for a building a quarter of a mile down the road. I had to hustle to get there.

Early in my consulting career, I showed up at a client's central location outside Washington, D.C., to teach a class, but the office was deserted. I didn't have a phone number for my contact person, a mistake I never made again (why do we learn so many important lessons from our mistakes?). It turned out the course was being held at a conference facility about eight miles away. Unfortunately, no one had informed me. I only had the address for the company's main office, so that's where I went. One employee just happened to stop by the main office and gave me a ride to the training location. If she hadn't appeared, I'd probably still be waiting there today.

I had a similar experience just last year. This time I had phone numbers, but none of the three contacts I tried to reach the morning of the class answered their phone. A helpful receptionist did her best to figure out where the class might be held, to no avail. The location had been changed, and again no one had informed me. A student in the class wandered by the reception area and recognized me, so I made it to the room eventually. This is pretty frustrating. And the three contact people for whom I left voice mails never replied to me at all. Weird.

Presentation Tip #11: Take backups. I have my PowerPoint presentation on my laptop, a copy of the file on a flash drive that I carry separately from the laptop bag, and another copy stashed in a private folder on my website. Any cloud storage, like Dropbox or iCloud, will work if you don't have your own website.

The flash drive is in case my laptop dies, gets lost, or is stolen, or if it doesn't get along with the presentation room's projector and I need to use a different computer. I always save the PowerPoint file with fonts embedded, as another random computer might lack some fonts you use. The cloud backup is in case all else fails. You can't have too many backups.

It's also a good idea to carry electronic backups of any handouts that are supposed to be distributed with your presentation. I have occasionally had problems with conferences where I'm speaking losing my materials. I always turn in my materials for duplication well before the deadline. But one conference where I was a regular speaker lost track of those files from time to time. Then they would follow up very late to remind me to send them my materials, which I had already done. That made me nervous.

One year I double-checked with the conference staff to ensure that they had received the file I had sent them, a sizable handout for my full-day tutorial. No problem, the person I spoke to replied; we have everything right here and they all look fine. But when I arrived at the conference site, a different staff member asked me, "Did you bring your handouts with you? We never received the materials for your tutorial."

I was pretty ticked about this. I explained the background situation and that I had confirmed their receipt of the handout materials. The staff member looked around on their network and said, "Oh, yes, there's your file. Now I remember. It was in some format we couldn't read."

I replied that the person I had spoken to months earlier had assured me she could open my file just fine. This staff member double-clicked on my file. It opened up and displayed correctly.

"What more do you want from me?" I asked with annoyance. How frustrating that was, particularly because I had so carefully followed up after my multiple previous problems. Fortunately, they were able to get the materials printed and delivered to my room only a half-hour late. I never delivered a tutorial at that conference again. They just weren't worth the hassle.

Presentation Tip #12: Don't be nervous if a lot of people attend your webinar. My webinars typically draw eight hundred to twelve hundred registrants, although only about 40 percent of them attend. That's a pretty large audience. However, from the speaker's perspective the experience of delivering a webinar is identical whether I have one attendee or one million. I'm just talking into the phone to whoever happens to be listening on the other end. The only difference might be how many questions you get. But you are only going to have a certain amount of time for Q&A, so you can only answer a few questions anyway, no matter how many people submit them.

While it can be intimidating to think of your message going out to a lot of people at once, when you're giving a presentation over the web it really doesn't feel like there's a large audience out there. So don't let that faceless crowd daunt you the way it could if you were staring from a podium out over a vast live audience.

I find these twelve tips help keep me confident, comfortable, and poised when I'm speaking in public. I'll bet they'll help you too.

Chapter 26

Some Presentation Tricks I Have Learned

Since I began giving professional presentations more than twenty-five years ago, I've picked up a number of useful techniques. Some of these I figured out on my own; others came from observing other presenters or hearing their suggestions. These tricks might help you deliver more effective presentations.

Open big

As soon as the spotlight shines, your immediate challenge is to gain the audience's attention, to get them on your side so they're receptive to your message. Try to think of an opening for your talk that will get the audience smiling and nodding in agreement immediately. Then they're on board for the rest of the show.

I begin several of my talks with a short audience survey. I list ten typical problem areas that frequently occur in the domain of my presentation, be it on software requirements, process improvement, or something else. I ask the audience members to note which of these problems they've experienced on their projects. Then, by show of hands, I ask who has experienced none of the problems I described, then one, and so on up through all ten.

Because these are such ubiquitous problems, I know that many people in the audience can relate to them. That is, they start nodding along with me from the very beginning of my talk. We've created a bond of common experience, forged a bit of rapport. I think this helps make the audience members receptive to my suggestions for addressing those all-too-common project challenges, which then constitute the rest of the presentation.

Colorful flip charts

In some presentations, I write items on a flip chart, such as ideas and comments contributed by the audience during a group discussion. I picked up a useful technique from a woman I saw doing this at a conference. She used two markers, alternating the colors as she wrote each item on the paper. This makes the contents of the flip chart easier to read, as the items don't all blur together visually. I now use this simple but effective technique all the time.

Humor doesn't hurt

Okay, I admit it, a lot of the material I present in my courses and short talks is pretty dry. It's difficult to make topics like project management, process improvement, and software requirements entertaining. So I try to incorporate a bit of levity, as humor livens up even the dullest material.

Over the years I've accumulated a bunch of random one-liners. They just popped out of my mouth at some point and gained a chuckle from the audience, so I keep them in. For instance, when I'm introducing myself at the beginning of a course, I often say, "I started out in life as a research chemist. Actually, I started out as a small child, but then I quickly became a research chemist." I know, this kind of material is not going to get me on Comedy Central. But audiences find it amusing, and it helps us get comfortable with each other. Smiling people are more receptive to your message.

Everyone can relate to cartoons, but avoid showing overused, trite, offensive, or excessive numbers of cartoons. Also, unless you drew it yourself, someone else likely owns the copyright to your cartoon. Be careful about incorporating copyrighted material of any kind into your presentation without citing the original source, procuring permission to use it, and possibly paying a licensing fee. Respect others' material as you would have them respect yours.

Quiet questioners

An audience member once asked a speaker a question from the front row of a large room. The questioner was speaking too quietly for people in the back of the room to hear. I noticed that as the speaker listened to the question, he slowly walked *away* from the questioner.

The speaker's body language indicated that he was listening attentively. Perhaps unconsciously, the questioner began speaking more loudly as the speaker grew more distant. This made it easier for other members of the audience to hear the question. I'm not sure if the speaker took that little walk deliberately, but it seemed like a good idea to me. Now, whenever I'm in a similar situation, I do the same thing. Most people really do start speaking louder as they see you moving away. Subtle, but effective.

Unless you're confident everyone in the room could hear the question, the audience will appreciate it if you repeat or paraphrase it. You usually have voice amplification available; the questioners do not. Reiterating the question also gives you a few seconds to think about the answer, or perhaps to reframe the question into one you'd prefer to answer. Politicians are masters of that last technique. I've never yet heard one answer a simple yes-or-no question with a simple yes or no.

Let's get moving

Listening to a presentation is a passive activity. It's easy for your attention to wander, to drift into a daydream, or even to nod off into slumber. And it's even worse for the audience. (Sorry; see "Humor doesn't hurt" above.)

One way to combat this as a speaker is to encourage the audience members to interact from time to time, either with you or with one another. Sometimes, I will ask them to spend a few moments talking among themselves about a particular topic and then share their small group's thoughts with the rest of the audience.

I also conduct quick surveys periodically. I might describe a particular technique in a class and then ask, "Have any of you tried this?" followed by, "How did it work for you?" This gets at least some of them moving their bodies a bit with a show of hands and perhaps a contribution to the discussion.

I have some ulterior motives here as well. These informal and totally unscientific surveys help me calibrate the audience's past experience and knowledge. If I describe an unfamiliar technique and a skeptical audience member sees that some other people around her have tried it, maybe my suggestion doesn't seem so strange. It's not just Karl's wacky scheme anymore. She might even ask one of those people who raised his hand to share his experience with the practice at the next break.

Audiences often have particular trouble remaining engaged right after lunch. While I schedule breaks in my full-day classes about every ninety minutes, I will often invite the attendees to take a one-minute stretch break halfway through that interval in the first session of the afternoon. They can stand up, loosen up, and wake up just enough to make it through the next chunk of the class until we take a real break.

Door prizes

When I'm delivering a presentation at a conference or a professional society meeting I will sometimes give away door prizes. These could be a copy of one of my books, a CD of one of my e-learning courses, or some other product. Giving away such prizes is a way to advertise my products and services, including the nontechnical books I've written.

Here's a trick I've come up with. If the lucky winner is several rows back in the audience, I hand the item to someone in the front row and ask him to pass it back. This way several people have a chance to touch and look at the item, which might stimulate their interest in it.

Other random tips from the experts

Over the years I've heard many tips from experienced speakers about how to deliver effective presentations or training courses.

Below, in no particular order and in their own words, are some of the suggestions I've heard from numerous experts, including Richard Bender, Frank Galea, Capers Jones, Howard Podeswa, and Ed Weller.

- Show actual data. The speaker evaluations I have seen as a speaker or program chair were better when presentations included data with sufficient discussion or interpretation.
- I use language and metrics that evoke memorable images in the audience's mind. This is especially important if you are presenting by audio only. For example, yesterday our Corporate Controller gave an update by audio-only conference call on Dodd-Frank financial reform. To convey the scope and breadth of the legislation, he created some visual imagery around the page count (2,300+) of the legislation and compared that size to past landmark reforms of various lengths.
- Some of the topics I teach are inherently dry, so I use historical analogies to liven them up a bit. For example, in discussing quality assurance strategies I'll mention the QA programs of the Roman Empire and the Danish navy in 1600. I then tie them to what people do today, what works, and what does not. These stories and images help the attendees understand and remember the key points I'm trying to make.
- I begin each class by asking the attendees what their expectations are for the class or what project issues they've encountered related to the class topic. I solicit this in an open-ended manner so as not to bias what they come up with. I write these down on a flip chart page and keep this list visible for the duration of the class, revisiting it periodically to see how we're doing. This list of expectations allows us to tie the course materials to the issues that most concern the students.
- Exercises can enhance any learning experience. All of the examples and exercises in our courses are taken

from real projects, scrubbed to protect the guilty and preserve confidentiality. Real-world examples do not work out as tidily as made-up ones. However, that is what students will run into once they return to their projects. The exercises are a blend of individual and team efforts.

- Look for ways to illustrate concepts with images and video clips, instead of just loads of textual bullet points. Look for the emotional connection to an issue and find an image that conveys that and helps the listener remember.
- Lately I've been trying something revolutionary: ditch the PowerPoint. It's amazing how not using slides immediately puts me more in touch with the mood in the room, keeps me and the students more engaged, and allows me to better pace the presentation in tune with the energy and needs of the students. It's like throwing away a crutch.

The next time you attend a presentation that you enjoy, reflect on what aspects of the speaker's style and approach kept your attention. Then look for ways to incorporate those same desirable characteristics into your own presentations. You'll be a more comfortable, confident, and competent speaker in no time.

Part 6

Writing Your Way to Success

Chapter 27

You Are What You Write

I wrote my first computer magazine article in 1984, not many years after what were then called microcomputers first appeared on the scene. Back then, we early adopters were all just trying to learn how the things worked and how to get them to do something interesting, useful, or amusing. I figured out how to use a fairly complex feature of my new computer. It occurred to me that other people also might find my newly-gained insight valuable, so I wrote an article. A magazine bought it. I began to write more articles about a wide variety of computing topics; I haven't stopped yet.

The ability to communicate effectively in writing is an essential skill for consultants. Much of the consulting work I've done has involved developing process-related materials for clients. I have created all manner of procedures, document templates, checklists, guidance documents, and the like. Other engagements have involved performing a process or document assessment that resulted in a written report of my observations and recommendations.

As you gain experience and wisdom in a particular domain, you might wish to share what you've learned with others through articles, conference papers, blog posts, or books. I've now written more than 160 articles on numerous software development, quality, and management topics, as well as more than 20 articles on organic chemistry and military history, of all things. Traditional print magazines published most of these articles, although more and more have appeared in recent years on websites. Most magazines will pay for articles; many websites will not.

But as we learned in Chapter 16, everything is negotiable. If you have a good enough story to tell and enough credibility in the industry, you might be able to negotiate some payment from anyone who publishes your work. In broad terms, you might get between $100 and $1,000 per article. Chapter 29 provides many recommendations regarding writing for magazines, websites, and blogs.

Eventually you might decide to write a book. That's a whole different proposition from writing a set of magazine articles or blog posts. Telling a story in a few thousand words on a focused topic isn't too hard. Writing sixty to one hundred thousand words in a typical book takes considerable planning, time, and effort. By way of calibration, this book is about sixty-seven thousand words long.

Then there's the whole matter of getting the book published, negotiating contracts, promoting it, and all the rest. It ain't trivial. Chapters 30 and 31 are devoted to suggestions about writing and publishing books. If you decide to go the self-publishing route, you might find the information in Chapter 32 helpful.

Many nonfiction books result from collaboration between two or more co-authors. I've tried this a couple of times. The first attempt was a complete failure. I quickly discovered that the man who had invited me to co-author the book with him expected me to do all the writing, based largely on his material, while he would review what I wrote. Unfortunately, he didn't review my drafts expeditiously, which hampered my ability to move the project along. That partnership lasted just two chapters before I bailed out. In contrast, my second co-authoring experience, many years later, was a grand success, as I describe in Chapter 33.

Choosing a role model

To get things started, here's one tidbit of wisdom I've acquired: think about whose writing you find particularly appealing and learn from them. You might have favorite authors whom you find to be especially helpful, interesting, and enjoyable to read. Take the time to study their work and assess *why* you like their writing. Then you can try to emulate some of those characteristics in your own work.

Many years ago, I realized that Steve McConnell was one of my favorite software authors; he's also a good friend now. Steve has written numerous top-selling software books and is esteemed in the software industry. When I thought about it, I realized that Steve uses fairly short sentences in much of his writing, and he writes in a direct, conversational style. I also favor that informal writing style, although I confess to being somewhat long-winded by nature. My sentences can get wordy. I also tend to overuse adverbs, and I say "tend to" a lot. We all have our shortcomings. But Steve's acclaimed writing gave me a goal to strive for.

Focusing on clarity

Once I recognized what I liked about Steve's writing, I tried to steer my own style in that direction. I use the statistics from Microsoft Word's grammar checker (part of the spell check feature) to provide guidance. I find the grammar checking feature in Word quite useless overall—I think it was programmed on Opposite Day—but I do like these statistics.

The grammar statistics report the average numbers of sentences per paragraph in the document, words per sentence, and characters per word. The average number of characters per word should be around five when writing in English. I aim to keep the average words per sentence no higher than twenty and preferably fewer. Shorter words, sentences, and paragraphs all enhance readability.

The statistics report also shows several readability measures. The higher the Flesch Reading Ease index, the easier the document is to read (duh). I aim for at least forty. The lower the Flesch-Kincaid Grade Level, the easier the document is to read. I keep my technical writing at a grade level of twelve. For nontechnical writing, I aim for a grade level of eight or nine. I also like to keep the number of passive sentences low. Sentences written in the active voice are more direct and easier to understand than passive sentences.

If the statistics don't come out like I want, I'll do some editing to simplify the material and increase the readability. By way of example, here are the statistics for this chapter:

- 1660 words
- Average of 4.3 sentences per paragraph (fine)
- Average of 15.2 words per sentence (fine)
- Average of 4.8 characters per word (typical)
- Two percent passive sentences (okay)
- Flesch Reading Ease of 58.1 (great)
- Flesch-Kincaid Grade Level of 8.7 (perfect)

If these statistics are meaningful, you should find this chapter easy to read. I hope that's the case.

Acquiring the information

During our professional careers, we each accumulate a store of knowledge and experience in various areas. It takes a certain type of skill to be able to synthesize the accumulated knowledge—particularly from multiple domains—and deliver it to readers in a way they find appealing and accessible. Technical information can be dull as dishwater. It helps to brighten it up with bits of thoughtfully-selected humor and personal experiences.

My technical books and articles include many true-life stories. These anecdotes make the content more tangible to the reader. When a reader can relate to an actual experience—pleasant or not—the point you're making comes across as more real and hence more meaningful. Every experience story in this book is true.

I've collected countless stories from my clients, who shared with me their challenges, frustrations, and successes. After relating one unhappy story a client said, "Gee, I hope that won't end up in your next book."

"Sure it will," I replied. "Where do you think I get all these stories? I don't make them up; I collect them."

Of course, I anonymize all such stories. I believe it's not important how we learn a lesson—from doing something silly, from forgetting to do something important, or from a flash of brilliance—so long as we absorb, apply, and share the insight.

Developing a style

The whole point of writing is to communicate with your readers. Readers respond to writing they don't have to work hard to understand. They love direct, simple tutorials that teach them techniques they can apply immediately. Readers appreciate clearly explained concepts, examples, and opinions.

Some authors write as though they want their readers to know how smart they are, using big words and convoluted phrasing. Nobody cares how smart you are. They just care if you're able to communicate useful information to them. Hence, my interest in using a simple and conversational writing style.

When I was writing a series of tutorials on assembly language programming for a computer magazine long ago, I met a fan who told me, "When I work through your articles, I feel like you're standing there explaining them to me." This is exactly the kind of reaction I'm hoping for when I write. It was great to hear that at least one person felt like I was communicating through the written word in just the way I wanted to.

As you develop your writing style, you might think about what kind of compliments from an admiring reader would mean the most to you. Then you can work to develop a style that elicits that sort of feedback. Just this week, a reader commented on one of my blog posts: "I always enjoy your articles as they provide so much insight and information in a simple and interesting way. I find that your books are also very user-friendly and practical." This comment delighted me. Words like simple, interesting, user-friendly, and practical were music to my ears. It's one thing to inspire people with ideas, but I'm most interested in giving busy practitioners both useful techniques and the motivation to apply them.

I was educated as a scientist. The first major document I wrote was my PhD thesis in physical organic chemistry, "Kinetics and Mechanism of Lithium Aluminum Hydride Reductions of Ketones." (What could be more fascinating than that? Actually, it was pretty cool.) Scientists neither write nor speak like normal people. When I began writing on topics other than chemistry, it took me some time to un-learn how scientists write, to revamp my writing style to be more accessible.

One of the best compliments I ever got on my writing was from someone who said, "You don't write like you have a PhD." I was most pleased.

Chapter 28

Four Eyes Are Better Than Two

One of the most powerful tools available to help you become a better writer is peer review. I cannot overstate the importance of having selected individuals carefully critique what you write before you inflict it on an unsuspecting world. As I reflected on how I learned to write, I realized that I benefited greatly from a few college professors who took the time to give me detailed critical feedback on papers I had written. By studying that feedback, I learned how to write better papers the next time.

Preparing a piece for publication involves at least four steps: your own review and self-editing, peer review, outside editing, and proofreading. No matter how brilliant a writer you think you are, a good editor will make you look better. Even when I write something that seems clean and focused to my eye, reviewers and editors always find small mistakes and ways to improve the delivery. In this chapter I'll explain the different types of reviewing and editing activities and their importance.

Take a look yourself

The first quality improvement round is your own critical review. After I've written a new article, book chapter, or blog post, I set it aside for at least a full day before I review it. Longer is better. If you re-read something immediately after writing it you don't really review it—you mentally recite it. I like to let my memory of the piece decay for a while so I can look at it with fresh, less biased eyes. Sometimes, I will then see sentences that make me wonder what in the world I was thinking when I wrote them.

When I'm looking over my writing, occasionally I hear a little nagging voice (just one voice, fortunately). It says, "That part doesn't work—redo it or cut it out."

I used to reply to myself, "Let's see how the reviewers feel about it." The reviewers invariably spotted that bit and hated it. I've learned to trust that little voice and to fix the awkward chunk right away. The voice hasn't been wrong yet.

Being naturally wordy, I use a little technique to help me tighten my writing. Each time I make an edit pass through an article or a chapter of a few thousand words, I try to remove one hundred words. I don't always achieve that goal. However, a constant focus on tightening the writing helps me deliver the maximum value per sentence to the reader. You'd be surprised how much you can take out and still say everything you want.

Use your word processor's tools to help find errors. Run spell check. Search for double periods. Replace any double spaces with single spaces following periods and colons or between words. Globally replace all single and double quotes with themselves to make sure they are all styled as curly ("smart") quotes. Make sure your headings, the body of the text, and references are all styled consistently. Run grammar check and see if any of the potential errors it reports do require correction. Run spell check again after making edits, as it's so easy to introduce a typo when you change something.

Enlisting other eyes

Once the piece is in good shape to your own eyes, it's time to send it to your peer reviewers. These reviewers are also called beta readers. The peer review process varies depending on what kind of work you're writing. Even if the piece is informal, I recommend asking at least one person to look it over. I would rather have a trusted colleague point out a typo, garbled sentence, or factual error than to have a website visitor or a prospective customer spot it. It's always a little embarrassing when someone finds a mistake in my work. But when a friendly reviewer detects it early on, I think of that as a "good catch."

Tough peer reviews are the most useful kind. They aren't much fun to read, but they sure help improve whatever you write. I've been fortunate in this regard. For each of my technical books, I have had a few—never more than three—reviewers who just didn't let me get away with anything.

Once I figure out who those reviewers will be on a particular writing project, I always dread receiving their feedback. I know I'll feel like an idiot, and I'll have to spend a lot of time processing their comments and reworking the piece. However, I also know that their input will greatly improve my work. Other reviewers just rubber-stamp what I send them as being fine, point out only minor typos, or don't respond at all. While I appreciate my beta readers' time and their glowing feedback, this kind of input just isn't of much help.

I've observed that reviewing nonfiction writing typically makes a document longer, whereas editing makes it shorter. Reviewers often suggest that I add more content, another example, or a figure to illustrate a point. By the time I've addressed all the reviewer input, the piece is perhaps 10 to 20 percent longer than the original version. So then it's time to go back to my remove-one-hundred-words philosophy to tighten it up again, particularly if I'm writing against a length limit. Good copy editing also will fix wordiness, repetition, redundancies, duplication, and saying the same thing multiple times.

Peer review is painful. You wrote the best piece you possibly could, you're proud of it, and you're eager to share it with others. It hurts when some of those other people don't respond as positively as you hope or recommend major revisions. You have to learn to accept the critical input in the spirit in which it's intended.

Quite naturally, authors get their egos tied up with their writing. As an author, you need to set your ego aside enough to be receptive to the input. Reviewers also must set their egos aside. A good reviewer will show respect for the effort the author put into the piece and will provide thoughtful, constructive feedback. The broad comment "This sucks," even if true, is not helpful. I've been passionate about peer reviews for a long time, even to the extent of writing a book titled *Peer Reviews in Software: A Practical Guide*.

Recently a friend and colleague I have known for more than ten years asked if I would review a short e-book she had written. I agreed, although I wasn't really a devotee of the topic she was addressing. I gave her quite detailed and frank feedback on both the content and the structure of her book, as that's the kind of input I always welcome most from my reviewers. Alas, I fear she was offended by my frankness. She referred to it as "harshness."

Certainly, I did not plan to offend her, nor did I feel I was being unduly harsh. I was just very direct, which I thought was appropriate with someone whom I knew fairly well. I don't know how many of my suggestions she will take, but quite honestly I don't feel that my review feedback was out of line. I was blunt but not—in my opinion—insulting. I'm sorry she took my input that way, as I never intend to offend. I'll be more careful next time.

We all want to be told how wonderful our writing is. The sad fact is that sometimes it's not. Different reviewers will come at what you've written from different perspectives and with varying expectations. As the author, you're always welcome to disregard any input a reviewer might provide. But I suggest you think about the point being made before you dismiss it.

Another colleague has invited me to review several of his book manuscripts over the years. They were in my main technical area, and he was a good guy who knew his stuff, so I agreed. I gave him extensive and detailed feedback on the first two books. But then I realized that he was making virtually none of the changes I suggested. My conclusion was that my perspective didn't align well with his, so I declined his invitations to review subsequent manuscripts; my efforts would have been wasted.

Copy editing

If you're writing articles for print or online magazines, you'll be dealing with one or more editors. The copy editor's job is to correct errors in spelling, grammar, and punctuation and to ensure the consistency and clarity of expression of your work. A copy editor probably won't make substantial content adjustments or suggest structural changes. The copy editor will ensure that your piece conforms to the magazine's house style standards for formatting and other conventions. For instance, consider the placement of a comma before the conjunction in an in-line list: "We vacationed in Germany, France, and Luxembourg." The comma after France is called the Oxford, or serial, comma. The house style at some magazines decrees use of the Oxford comma; others don't use it. I like the clarity that final comma provides.

The definitive reference for many copy editors is *The Chicago Manual of Style*. I keep a copy handy and refer to it when I'm not certain how to express something. For example, if you're referring to a time in the morning, which abbreviation do you use: AM, A.M., am, a.m., or something else? Should "20" be shown as numerals or be written out? *Chicago* will tell you.

When writing a book, a traditional publisher generally will engage either an in-house or freelance copy editor (possibly along with an artist, a compositor, and an indexer, depending on the book). It's a good idea to build a collaborative relationship with your editor. You really have to learn to respect the editing process. Conversely, the editor needs to understand your preferences, respect your style, and deal considerately with your hot buttons. A good editor will preserve your "voice" even as she hones your message.

You're not obligated to accept every change the editor suggests. Nonetheless, you should carefully consider each proposed change. Most of them are no-brainers: accept the change. Ultimately, though, the author's name, not the editor's, goes on the byline, so you are the final authority on what gets published.

Good editing makes a big difference in how a sharp-eyed reader perceives a publication. For some reason, I'm quite good at spotting typographical and word usage errors (which is not to say that my own work is flawless; it rarely is). When I find these mistakes in a published book, they annoy me. When I was writing my first book years ago and starting to think about seeking a publisher, I realized that several software books I had read from one publisher were replete with errors. The editing looked sloppy to me. Although that publisher did offer me a contract for my book, I declined it for that very reason. Fortunately, the editors I ultimately worked with were fantastic. The text is error-free.

One of the most common mistakes I see in books these days is the incorrect use of homophones, words that sound alike but are spelled differently: write, right, rite. The reader doesn't care whether these errors originated with the author or not. A published book riddled with such mistakes is an indication of inadequate editing and proofreading, and only your name is on the cover.

Developmental editing

Your publisher might have a developmental editor work with you, particularly if you're not an experienced author. A developmental editor will propose more radical changes than will a copy editor. This is particularly helpful if your manuscript is not well structured or well organized, or if the manuscript has technical shortcomings you must address before it's ready to release.

The editors at Dorset House Publishing added enormous value to my first book, *Creating a Software Engineering Culture*, by performing two stages of editing. First, developmental editing helped me transform a poorly structured, flabby manuscript into a much more effective vehicle for telling my story. Second, copy editing greatly cleaned up and tightened my prose and presentation. I lost twenty thousand words of text along the way—words I had spent many hours crafting to the best of my ability—but it was a far better book after the surgery. This experience gave me an intimate appreciation of the phrase "cutting-room floor."

Given that the traditional publishing business has changed considerably in recent years, a book publisher probably would not be so accommodating today. Publishers are looking for manuscripts in near-complete form, ones they don't have to massage much before going to press. You'll have a much better chance of selling your book to a publisher if it's already in very good shape.

Therefore, if you are not an experienced author, consider hiring a professional editor on your own to help polish your work before you send the manuscript to a publisher. That investment might make the difference between a rejection letter and a shiny new book with your name on it in your office.

Check it carefully

With both articles and books, be sure to read the edited version carefully to make sure that editing did not introduce inadvertent changes. This happens all the time. On one of my very earliest articles, I was surprised to see an error in the published article that wasn't in my manuscript. I had said "flak," but the magazine printed "flack." These words have very different meanings. Mine was right.

That experience opened my eyes to the realization that when you think the author has made a mistake, an editor might have actually introduced it. Making corrections in text can easily generate additional errors. For this reason, I always request to do a quick proofread of the final copy before it goes to press.

My worst editing experience took place on a magazine article of about four thousand words. The freelance copy editor told me he did a light edit. However, his modifications changed the meaning of what I was trying to say in no fewer than twenty-six places! For instance, I was presenting a case study, and I wrote, "We did A, and then we did B." The editor thought it read more smoothly as, "We did B, and then we did A." But it was a case study—that wasn't what we did. You have to proofread very carefully to catch those kinds of issues. The editor is not an expert in your domain—you are. It might not be obvious to the editor that a small change can disrupt the meaning of your message.

Rarely, you might find that you and the copy editor just don't click. I experienced that problem on one of my books. The editor was introducing too many errors, changing my voice too much, and generally adding little value. After giving it enough time to be sure I wasn't overreacting, I shared my frustration with the overall project editor. He then took over the copy editing responsibility himself and did a superb job. Nearly all of the editors I've worked with have been excellent, though, and I'm grateful for the countless improvements they made in my writing. Learn from the input you get from editors so you can do a better job the next time.

A friend who's a highly experienced editor offered the following wisdom: "For new or first-time writers, working with any editor on staff can be touchy. If they don't like the editor and want him removed, they will need to be very tactful with the editor's supervisor. Another tip: be really nice to anyone you work with on the publishing team. Lowly copy editors sometimes become acquisitions editors and project editors, or they move on to bigger publishing houses and websites. Forming a good relationship with your editors can work to your advantage."

This is first-class advice. When I met this woman, she had just started as a copy editor at a magazine devoted to software development. Within a few years, she had risen to the top position on the masthead, Editor in Chief. We worked together very well and got along well also. That's a nice plus.

A professional book copy editor will typically build a style sheet as he goes along. The style sheet will list items such as names that appear in the work, proper nouns, specialized terms, jargon, and any expressions that might be punctuated or spelled in a specific way. One of my books discusses something called a dialog map. "Dialog" can be spelled this way or as "dialogue." It's important for the editor to know—and remember—which of those alternatives the author wishes to use. Maybe in some places the author used the term "login" and in others she used "log in," "logon," and "sign in." The style sheet helps the copy editor ensure consistency throughout the book.

Proofreading

Editing isn't the end of the pre-publication process. You still need to proofread the final copy, be it an article or a book. This is a different type of activity than editing. You're not looking to improve the piece further but rather to make sure it's in final form, free from errors, and ready to present to your loyal readers.

Ideally, the proofreader and the editor will be different people. I always proofread the final copy myself as well, but of course, I'm already very close to it. The closer you are to the material, the harder it is to spot errors. I encountered an example of this just recently in my first novel, *The Reconstruction*. A sharp-eyed reader pointed out a typographical error that I had not seen on the multiple proofreading passes I had made after editing was complete.

If you can, line up an independent proofreader, in addition to scrutinizing the piece yourself. But even that approach offers no guarantees. Another reader called my attention to a second error in *The Reconstruction* that had been present in the manuscript from my very first draft. I never caught that mistake on my approximately fifteen passes through that chapter. But I didn't feel too bad, because neither did my twenty-one beta readers, my copy editor, nor my two proofreaders. But it's wrong, it's my responsibility, and I will fix it.

People use a variety of techniques to proofread their own text. As I suggested earlier, setting it aside for a few days helps. You can read the copy line by line, looking just at the words and punctuation instead of their meaning. Some people use a piece of paper to cover all of the text except for the one line they're proofreading. Others read the text aloud, which is far slower but also meticulous. A proofreader might wish to refer to the style sheet the copy editor created to ensure that any specialized words or names appear the same way each time they occur.

Another technique is to read the text backwards sentence by sentence or paragraph by paragraph. This will help you focus on the content, rather than getting caught up with the story and just flowing along. That's especially valuable if you are proofreading your own writing. You've already gone through it countless times, and your brain tends to recite it back to you, rather than letting you look at it fresh and catch subtle errors. Find a trick that works for you. You might be surprised at how many errors you spot. I always am.

Using speech-recognition software

For about twenty years I've done nearly all of my writing by voice, using Dragon NaturallySpeaking speech-recognition software. This software does quite a good job of recognizing what I say and typing it out for me. Once I got the hang of writing verbally I found it to be considerably faster than typing. It's also easier on my wrists and forearms, preventing repetitive strain injuries.

Speech-recognition software will never misspell a word. However, it sometimes misinterprets what I say, which results in text other than what I intended. Therefore, I need to proofread anything I write by voice more carefully than usual because spell check doesn't do me any good.

As I was proofreading this chapter, I found an error that resulted from exactly this type of speech misinterpretation. The text said "are" instead of my intended "or." Those two words do sound similar. Dragon NaturallySpeaking does a very good job at choosing the right word based on context, but it will never be perfect. Proofread vigorously!

When it's all your responsibility

If you elect to self-publish a book or write an e-book, you're on your own for copy editing and proofreading. Don't think you can do this yourself or just hand it over to a friend—professional editors are much better than us amateurs. My memoir of life lessons, *Pearls from Sand: How Small Encounters Lead to Powerful Lessons*, was not self-published, but I was responsible for supplying the publisher with the final manuscript, ready to print ("camera-ready"). Therefore, I had to line up a copy editor and a proofreader to make my manuscript as clean as possible.

I began by hiring my old friend Barbara Hanscome. I worked with Barbara on many articles while she was an editor at *Software Development* magazine. Now she does freelance editing. Barbara is the best editor I've ever worked with. As I expected, she did a terrific job on my book manuscript. She saved me from myself more times than I could count. I also hired a local Portland, Oregon, firm to do some of the copy editing and all of the proofreading. They too did an excellent job, as did an editor I recently hired through another Portland company called Indigo when I wrote my first novel, *The Reconstruction*. They were all worth every penny.

Chapter 29

Writing for Magazines, Websites, and Blogs

Many software magazines were published during the 1990s and early 2000s. Some of those have faded away, but there are plenty of websites that post articles on every aspect of software development and project management, as well as every other topic under the sun.

Writing for publication is a good way for consultants to gain visibility for their ideas and expertise. Since 1984, I've written articles for more than twenty software magazines and websites. Working with so many different outlets and editors has given me a good feel for how to prepare articles for publication.

Knowing your audience

If rule number one for effective writing is "know your subject," rule number two certainly is "know your audience." Before you submit an article, think carefully about what kind of people read that periodical or visit that website. Read previous articles so you have an idea of what topics, content, and writing styles appeal to the readers and—just as important—to the editor or site manager. Are the articles highly technical in nature, perhaps including code fragments or research data? Are they written in a conversational style or more formally? Are figures, diagrams, or tables commonly used? How are references cited, if at all? Are most of the articles how-to tutorials, opinionated essays, reports of industry trends, or what? Do the authors incorporate much humor in their pieces? How long are the articles on average? Do they ever publish multiple articles in a series? Are most of the authors opinion leaders or practitioners?

It's a good idea to make sure your article aligns with the content and format that people expect to find in a particular forum. You might be able to get some of this information from the periodical's writer's or submission guidelines.

Fitting in

I try hard to make my submissions look like a natural fit for a particular periodical. For instance, I always ask how many words the editor wants. Magazine articles typically range from fifteen hundred to four thousand words in length. Articles intended for website or blog publication are shorter, perhaps seven hundred to fifteen hundred words. A figure ordinarily is counted as two hundred words for space purposes.

If a magazine editor requests two thousand words, that's what he gets. If you submit a manuscript with three thousand words, it simply won't fit in the space the editor has in mind for it. The most likely outcomes are either rejection or substantial editing if he likes your story but needs something shorter. In rare cases you might persuade the editor to run a longer article as a series of shorter pieces, but don't count on it.

Through some amazing good fortune, I've managed to place every piece of writing I have ever submitted for publication. If the first magazine rejected my submission, I would modify it to fit in with the next one to which I submitted it. It occasionally took up to four attempts, but it always found a home.

It's not always necessary to submit a full manuscript. If you have an idea for an article, float it past an editor who you think might find it interesting and see if you get a nibble. If no one is interested, maybe you don't need to spend the time writing and polishing the piece. One year, I outlined a series of nine possible articles for one magazine. After the editor and I agreed on the topics, I began writing them at my convenience. The more you understand about the readership the magazine's editorial staff is targeting, the easier it is to get a proposal accepted.

Delighting the editor

My philosophy is to make the editor's job as easy as possible. I want her to sense immediately that my submission feels right for her periodical and audience. That's why I conform to the periodical's house style. As an example, if it's not customary for their articles to have sections titled Introduction or Conclusion, my submission won't contain them either. It's an old dictum that in an article or a presentation you "tell 'em what you're going to tell 'em, tell 'em, then tell 'em what you told 'em." That's not a bad policy, but you can do that without having sections mundanely titled Introduction and Conclusion.

I've always had the impression that the less work an editor has to do to turn your submission into a published article, the more favorably inclined she will be toward you in the future. For each of my professional interactions—an article, a book, a presentation, a consulting gig—my goal is for the other party to think, "I'd be happy to work with Karl again." Making an article require as little editing as possible is one step toward this outcome.

If you really want to get on an editor's bad side, missing deadlines will do it. Magazines come out on a fixed schedule, and websites have to deliver streams of fresh content; they aren't going to wait for your late article. I take great pride in having never missed a deadline for submitting an article, conference presentation materials, or a book manuscript.

Not everyone is like this though. More than one frantic editor has called me to ask if I could plug a hole in the magazine because some other contributor didn't deliver when promised. Editors will come back to you if they know they can count on you to deliver on time. Emergencies do arise, so if you find that you cannot meet a writing commitment, tell the affected parties as soon as possible so they can adjust. Going dark is the worst thing you can do.

Dangling the bait

Editors like catchy titles and captivating opening paragraphs. The editor might retitle the article to make it better fit the magazine's style or grab the reader's attention, so don't get overly attached to your initial title.

A clever title initiates the connection between author and audience. Some of my article titles promise a certain number of tidbits of wisdom: 7 deadly sins, 10 traps to avoid, 21 success tips. Other titles are intended to make the reader ask, "Hmm, I wonder what this is about?" Some examples are:

- "See You in Court" (about an engagement I had as an expert consultant for a party in a lawsuit)
- "When Telepathy Won't Do" (key practices in requirements development)
- "Know Your Enemy" (a tutorial on risk management)
- "Just Too Much to Do" (described a project prioritization spreadsheet tool)
- "Stop Promising Miracles" (about a project estimation technique)

Try to concoct a title that both accurately reflects what you're presenting and piques the reader's interest in just a few words.

Setting the hook

I work hard on the opening paragraph for each article. You have a very short window in which to get the reader's attention. If you don't engage readers with the first paragraph, it doesn't matter what you say in the rest of the article because they won't read it. And if the very first sentence doesn't grab them, the rest of the first paragraph doesn't matter either. Busy people aren't likely to forge ahead, patiently hoping the article gets interesting at some point. Make your opening catchy enough that a reader can't help but keep going.

I often start with something that will get the reader nodding in agreement with me from the outset, such as an indication that I feel the reader's pain and frustration. Here's an example:

> Software managers sometimes assume that every skilled programmer is also proficient at interviewing customers and

writing requirements, without any training, resources, or coaching. This isn't a reasonable assumption. Like testing, estimation, and project management, requirements engineering has its own skill set and body of knowledge.

Once readers get the idea that you understand their pain points and can offer some relief, then you can reel them in and wow them with your wisdom.

You have arrived!

If you establish a reputation for writing high-quality material, delivering on time, and stimulating reader interest, a magazine editor might even offer you a column. I was so excited in 1986 when I was invited to write a tutorial column on assembly language programming for a monthly computer magazine. I could write about anything I wanted, knowing that it would be published. Magazine editors aren't always thrilled about publishing a series of articles by the same author, but with a column I could address larger themes over a span of several articles. And I'd have a sustained income stream to boot. That was a lot of fun for two years.

Chapter 30

You Say You Want to Write a Book?

Consultants are the kind of people who like to share what they know (at a reasonable price), so many consultants get the notion of writing a book. They might already have been speaking at conferences, delivering courses, and writing articles or blogs; a book is the logical next step.

I've met a lot of people who said they were writing a book, planned to write a book, hoped to write a book, or wanted to have written a book. Most of them never do. I met a consultant in 1996 who told me he was co-authoring a book with another experienced writer. Periodically over the years he has said they were still working on their project. It hasn't appeared yet.

Most of the people I know who never quite finished a book didn't treat it as a project. At least in my experience, writing a book takes a lot of time. I usually spend about six months of significant effort writing each of my books, with additional time devoted to editing, revision, and proofreading during the production process. If you're serious about getting it done, you have to elevate it to a suitable priority in your work queue. This often means turning down paying work to free up time for the book. That's a tough decision for many consultants.

You also need to instill discipline into your writing approach. I know one author who sets aside several hours to write every morning, starting about 5 a.m. I've never taken that approach, but when I decide to write a book, I do carve out the necessary time to get it done. Other projects and amusements are put on hold for the duration. If you don't dedicate the time, it's won't happen.

An experienced author once told me, "It's an exciting day when you hold the first copy of your first book in your hand." He was absolutely right. It really was a thrill. And it never gets old, matter how many books I've written.

Why write a book?

If you see a book in your future, think about why you want to write it. Having books to your credit certainly looks good on a resume. They give you both credibility and visibility in your field. It's fun and exciting to be able to tell people about "my book." I get a lot of personal fulfillment and pride from having written multiple books—ten now, including this one. It's always a treat to hear people say they found my books useful and interesting.

Perhaps you want to write a book that you can include with classes you teach or to give away as a marketing tool to promote your company's services. Whatever your reason, keep it in focus as you structure the book and explore publishing alternatives, just as you would manage the vision and scope of a software project.

Sometimes, you feel that you just *have* to write a book to tell a story you're driven to share. That was the case with both my first software book and my first nontechnical book, a memoir of life lessons titled *Pearls from Sand*. I described this feeling to another aspiring author, saying, "There was a book inside of me that just had to get out." He stared at me as though I came from another planet. I guess he hadn't experienced that same emotion, although he professed a desire to write a book himself. I never learned what his motivation was.

I knew early in my software career that I wanted to write a book, but I wasn't sure what to write about. A little book-writing safety tip: having a clear topic in mind is a good starting point. Two events converged to lead me to my first book, *Creating a Software Engineering Culture*, which appeared in 1996. First, I had written an article by that same title in 1994 for *Software Development* magazine. More emails poured in after that one article than for all the other articles I've ever written—combined. "Hmmm," I said to myself, "perhaps there's something there."

Second, at about the same time, I happened to win a prize at a conference presentation, a copy of the speaker's book on software management. As I was reading the book on the airplane home, I said to myself, "I think I could write a better book than this." So I did. But it wasn't easy.

After I decided I was going to try to write a book I set myself five, somewhat fanciful, goals:

1. Write a book.
2. Write enough books that a reviewer might say, "In his latest book. . ."
3. Get well-known people to write cover blurbs (called "early praise") for my book.
4. Become well-enough known as an author that people ask me to write cover blurbs for *their* books.
5. Have my name appear in larger letters than the title on the cover.

I have now accomplished all but the fifth of those goals. Close enough! Let me share with you some insights I've picked up along the way.

How do you learn?

Where do you learn how to write a book? Nothing I studied in high school or college prepared me for that. Consequently, I really had no idea what I was doing when I embarked on Book #1. My inexperience showed in the original manuscript. One reason I'm writing *this* book is to help you avoid struggling as much as I did.

At a meeting of the Editorial Board for the journal *IEEE Software* one year, I sat down with two other experienced authors and compared notes. Among the three of us, we had published something like eleven well-received books by that time. We discovered that we all took different approaches to book-writing. Hearing how some other authors approach a book was illuminating.

I work best from a detailed outline that ensures I will meet my objectives for the project. In contrast, one of those other authors said, "When I conceived <Book X>, I didn't know exactly where I was going with it, so I just started writing and watched what happened." That free-form approach wouldn't work for me, but it served this respected author well on the innovative topic he was trailblazing. You'll need to figure out what writing method will work best for each of your own book projects. I'm still an outline guy.

My first draft of *Creating a Software Engineering Culture* left much to be desired. I began with a laughably skimpy outline, less than three pages for what turned into a nearly four hundred-page book. The result was a badly structured manuscript that had thirteen chapters of wildly varying length, countless long bullet lists, a lack of continuity, and numerous other problems.

Thanks to much valuable feedback from my very tolerant publisher, I was able to greatly improve the manuscript. It took a lot of effort that added little value to the content but a great deal to the presentation. I am forever indebted to Wendy Eakin and her colleagues at Dorset House Publishing for their patient and meticulous editing and guidance. The result was a nicely focused, cohesive book with a distinctive visual presentation and a well-received conversational tone that I've tried to maintain ever since.

So in my case, I learned a lot about writing books by writing a poor one and following many fine suggestions about how to write a better one. Perhaps that's the way most of us learn, but it wasn't enjoyable at the time.

Some book-writing recommendations

Writing my first book was a painful experience. As with so many painful experiences, it also afforded a powerful learning opportunity. Countless books on how to write books are available. You might check out *Weinberg on Writing: The Fieldstone Method* by Gerald M. Weinberg, a prolific and respected author.

Following are some things I've learned about book-writing. Perhaps not all of these will apply to every opus in your future, but they're all worth contemplating.

Structure. It's usually a good idea to organize a book into several parts containing groups of chapters on a common theme. At my editor's recommendation, I restructured the thirteen chapters in my initial draft of *Creating a Software Engineering Culture* into twenty chapters of more uniform length, grouped into six parts. This restructuring required a month of tedious drag-and-drop editing.

I learned my lesson. For my next book, the first edition of *Software Requirements*, I began with a much more carefully thought-out seventeen-page outline, with nineteen chapters in three parts. As a result, I had to do almost no restructuring along the way. This is analogous to designing your software before writing the code. I'm a big believer in working hard on your book's architecture. It's a lot faster, and less painful, to revise and iterate on an outline than on fully-written text. Trust me on this; I've done both.

Themes. It's important to have some threads of continuity—recurrent themes—running through the book. Tie sections of the book back to those themes, both to make sure the content you include is relevant and on-message, and to constantly reinforce those themes to the reader. You might be tempted to include certain material that intrigues you, but if it doesn't align with one of your book's themes, perhaps it just doesn't belong there.

I read the draft manuscript for one colleague's proposed first book and told her, "There are two and a half books in here. Figure out which one you're writing this time, and save everything else for later." She condensed it down and wrote a great book. Subsequently she put out others. Focus, focus, focus.

Sometimes, when I've read manuscripts by other authors, it seems that they've thrown in every thought, idea, and experience that they're excited about, regardless of whether it fits with the chapter or even with the book. To help avoid this tempting trap, here's one technique I use. I put just a few bullet points at the top of each chapter before I begin drafting it. These bullets remind me of the key messages I wish to impart in that chapter.

As I write, I refer back to that short list periodically to make sure I'm not including extraneous stuff just because I think it's interesting. I might adjust the focus of the chapter if I find that my initial intent wasn't quite right. Then, when the draft is done, I remove those temporary bullets because they've served their purpose of keeping me on track.

Hooks. Consider devising some "hooks," structured devices that give your book some memorable presentation patterns. You might study other books that you find appealing and see what distinctive characteristics they have that stick in your mind or make the content more accessible. Following are some hooks I've used or seen:

- Begin each chapter with a pithy quotation or a concise focal statement like the "pearl of wisdom" that opens each chapter of *Pearls from Sand*.
- Place icons in the margin to identify elements like "culture builders" and "culture killers," cross-references to other chapters, traps to avoid, and true experience stories.
- Include a summary of key points at the end of each chapter.
- Place an annotated bibliography at the end of each chapter.
- Append a list of next steps, practice activities, or worksheets to each chapter to help the reader begin applying the material.
- Embed true-life anecdotes in boxes or sidebars that reinforce the points made in the text.
- Incorporate original cartoons.
- Sprinkle pull quotes of key sentences throughout the text.
- Include a repeating or evolving visual element, such as a tab printed on the outside edge of each page that provides a "you are here" navigational aid.

Thinking about such design elements and getting a clear focus on the scope, objectives, and themes for my books help me write much more efficiently. One big benefit is needing far less rework than my first book demanded. There's no single correct way to write a book, of course, but this is the approach I find effective.

Writing a book is not easy. It takes dedication, persistence, and time. When I was doing my first book, while working full-time at Kodak, periodically I would call out to my wife. "Chris," I'd say, "would you come shoot me, please?"

One day she replied, "I'm about ready to." Not being totally stupid, I stopped asking.

As with everything else, writing books gets easier with practice. When I completed the manuscript for my second book three years later, I said to Chris, "That didn't go too badly."

"No," she said, "you didn't ask me to shoot you even once."

I guess that's progress.

Chapter 31

Getting Your Book into Print

Writing a book is one thing; making it available to the world is an entirely separate proposition. The world of book publishing has changed in recent years, as self-publishing and electronic books have skewed the economic value proposition for both authors and publishers. While today's author has other alternatives available, there are still numerous traditional publishers who look for high-quality, marketable manuscripts.

Once you've established a reputation as someone who can write books that sell, publishers are always happy to hear from you. Getting your foot in the door can be challenging though. For this reason, and many others, I'm deeply grateful to Wendy Eakin of Dorset House Publishing, who took a chance on a first-time author in 1995 and helped him learn the craft.

This chapter describes much of what I've learned about publishing books. No doubt other authors have had different experiences. I don't claim that this is the only way—or even necessarily the best way—to go about creating a book. It's just the approach I have taken for seven books on software development and management, as well as a memoir of life lessons and a novel.

My friend Scott Meyers created an extensive web page at http://www.aristeia.com/authorAdvice.html that's an excellent resource for the aspiring book author. Scott is a talented and prolific writer who is renowned for his expertise in the C++ programming language. He combined his own publishing experiences with input from numerous other book authors into this page. If you're thinking of writing a technical book, carefully read what Scott has to say, recognizing that the industry is evolving as we speak.

Even if you're able to get a book written and published, you shouldn't expect miracles. Don't quit your job and buy that beach house, expecting book royalties to keep you in margaritas for the rest of your life. I don't have any firm figures about industry sales, but here are my own heuristics. If your technical book sells five to ten thousand copies, you should be pleased that you created something your colleagues find useful. If you sell twenty-five thousand copies, you should be delighted. And if you exceed one hundred thousand copies with any book, you're in a small group of highly-regarded (and very happy) authors.

Targeting a niche

I once knew a consultant who envisioned publishing a large set of books on a particular subdomain of software engineering. He had already drafted numerous volumes in the series, which he distributed in his training courses. However, it's not easy to find a publisher who's interested in releasing such an extensive series of books by a single author in any specific niche.

As far as I know, this consultant never did get any of his books published. It's a shame, because he had a lot of great knowledge. I think he would have been better off to distill his vast quantity of material down into one or two focused, practical, and distinctive books in that area and then approach a publisher.

My writing approach has been to identify some area of software engineering that I felt was lacking an appropriate book and then attempt to plug that gap. At the time I wrote the first edition of *Software Requirements* in 1999, just a few practical books on requirements engineering were available. None covered the breadth of topics that I thought were important, so I took a stab at it. The result was a book of ninety thousand words that sold about forty-five thousand copies.

A few years later, I realized that I had accumulated quite a lot of additional material, much of it in response to questions that people had asked me about requirements. That extra material, along with many other enhancements, eventually led to the second edition (what publishers call a 2E) of *Software Requirements* in 2003. (A second edition is not the same thing as a second printing. A new edition contains significant revisions, whereas a new printing will, at most, correct minor errors.) This edition was sixty thousand words longer than the first; I guess I did have more to say on the topic. The 2E also sold well. I released a third edition in 2013, as described in Chapter 33, "On Co-Authoring a Book."

As another example of plugging a hole in the literature, I've long been a strong proponent of software peer reviews and inspections (a type of well-structured, formal peer review). My own software work was greatly improved by getting a little help from my friends through peer reviews. Some years ago there were several books in that niche already, but they were all hefty—350 to 450 pages—and they focused on the inspection technique, giving short shrift to other possible ways to perform reviews.

I didn't think the topic was complicated enough to require such imposing texts. So, in 2002 I wrote *Peer Reviews in Software: A Practical Guide*. It was just 230 pages long, covered several review techniques besides inspection, and added some fresh content on review metrics and how to install a review program into a software organization. I targeted this book at practitioners who were serious about software quality but might be daunted by a massive tome on inspection alone.

My recommendation is that you aim your book at a niche that isn't already well covered in the existing literature for your domain. You can drill down into a specialized area, synthesize related topics into a comprehensive overview, improve on the existing books in a particular field, or invent something entirely new.

A prospective publisher will assess how your proposal fits into the marketplace. Something that's going head-to-head against numerous similar titles could be a tougher commercial prospect than a book that stands alone or offers something distinctive.

Publishers don't simply print interesting or well-written books; they need to publish books that sell. Otherwise, they go out of business.

The elevator pitch

You step into an elevator in a big hotel and press the button for the twenty-fourth floor. During the ride, you chat idly with the elevator's other occupant, who is attending the same conference you are and is heading for the nineteenth floor. You just happen to casually mention that you're writing a book. "Cool," she says. "What's it about?" You have perhaps twenty seconds to tell this prospective customer just enough so she says as she departs, "Sounds interesting. I'll look for it when it comes out. Good luck."

This condensed summary of your book is called the elevator pitch or elevator story. The first time someone asked me what my book was about, I confess I was stumped. How do I distill a four hundred-page book into twenty seconds? This puzzlement was constructive though. It forced me to sit down and carefully think through just what my book *was* about and how I could quickly explain that to even a normal (i.e., non-software) person.

With practice, your elevator pitch will roll right off your tongue whenever you encounter a possible reader. For instance, here's the pitch for my first novel, *The Reconstruction*:

> When Jessica, a forensic sculptor, completes a facial reconstruction on unidentified remains found in a forest grave, she discovers that she has a shocking personal connection to the victim. Jessica is then driven to identify the victim, confirm their relationship, and deliver justice for her death.

Devise your elevator pitch early in the writing process. It will help keep your overriding objective and book themes in the front of your mind as you develop the contents. If you have an initial conversation or email exchange with a prospective publisher or literary agent, the elevator pitch is your first shot at piquing his interest.

Choosing a publisher

If you scan the spines of the books in your office, you'll see many publishers represented. As an author, you need to identify publishers who might be interested in your work and will do a good job of both producing the book and marketing it. Look for publishers that release titles that you like for both their content and their visual presentation.

Speaking of titles, don't get too emotionally committed to yours. The publisher might prefer an alternative title for marketing purposes. That's happened to me several times, not always to my liking. But they do get the final say.

Look for a publisher who might find your book to be a good addition to its portfolio. Large publishers often have several book series on various themes, so you might target your book for inclusion in a particular series. Several of my books are in the Microsoft Press Best Practices series. My book on software peer reviews is in Addison-Wesley's Information Technology series. If you can pitch your book as a logical fit for a particular series, the series editor might receive your proposal warmly.

Some of the biggest publishers in software are Addison-Wesley (an imprint of Pearson Education), McGraw-Hill, Microsoft Press, O'Reilly, Prentice Hall, and Wiley. There are many others. Dorset House has a long-standing reputation as a publisher of high-quality books. The Pragmatic Bookshelf is a relatively new publisher that has established an impressive portfolio of titles, mostly on programming topics. There are pluses and minuses with both large and small publishers. If you're just starting out as an author, you might get more personal coaching and guidance from a smaller publisher.

To help you select a candidate publisher, you might ask some authors you know who have published with a particular company about their experiences. Even if you don't know the authors except by reputation go ahead and write to them. Most software authors are nice people who are happy to help an aspiring writer.

I have always dealt with publishers directly, not through a literary agent. Referrals can be helpful to get you in the door. People sometimes approach me with book ideas and questions about publishers. If their project seems to have merit, I'm happy to introduce them to the publishers I've worked with.

I did seek an agent when I was trying to publish my memoir of life lessons, *Pearls from Sand*, because I had no contacts in the self-help publishing world. I didn't end up with an agent after all, although one I queried did point me toward the publisher who ultimately accepted the book.

If you're dealing with a small publisher, your initial point of contact might be one of the principals of the company. When dealing with a larger publisher, you'll work first with an acquisitions editor (AE). The AE is responsible for evaluating ideas and proposals and landing promising projects. Publishers need authors as much as authors need publishers, so don't be shy about approaching a publisher with your idea, proposal, outline, or manuscript.

Opinions vary as to whether it's appropriate to submit the same manuscript or proposal to multiple publishers concurrently. I think it's fine, so long as you don't get carried away. That is, I think it's reasonable to submit your book concurrently to a few candidate publishers for whom you think it would be a good fit. However, I wouldn't broadcast it to every publisher of software books in the universe, hoping for at least one hit.

The proposal

You begin with an idea, a title, and maybe an elevator pitch. If you want a publisher to give your idea due consideration, you'll need to submit a full proposal. Once you've identified candidate publishers, peruse their websites for templates or suggested outlines for their preferred proposal format. If you've spoken to an acquisitions editor or other contact person, they can describe what they want to see in a proposal. Whether dealing with an agent or a publisher, follow their requested submission form and content carefully.

If all else fails, there's some standard information you should include in your proposal, which I will describe in this section. You can see the proposals I submitted for several of my books at https://tinyurl.com/goingitalone. I'm not saying they're the best proposals ever, but each of them did lead to a contract.

Once you've identified yourself and your position in the proposal, present a concise overview of the proposed book. Explain why the world needs it. Describe its major characteristics and the value proposition for the reader. Include a synopsis of the topics you intend to cover, either in narrative form or as a high-level outline. The publisher doesn't necessarily need to see the full outline that you might have developed to guide your writing, but he wants to know your topics and how you anticipate organizing them.

Estimate the final word count for the book and the approximate number of figures and tables you expect to include. By way of calibration, a two hundred-page technical book probably contains around sixty thousand words. My *Software Requirements, 3rd Edition* book with co-author Joy Beatty contains 245,000 words that fill nearly 650 pages. Word counts are more meaningful than page count estimates, as fonts and formatting have a huge impact on how many words will fit on a page.

In another section you might itemize the outstanding features of the book, including any hooks you've devised that would give the book a distinctive look and feel. If you plan to set up a website with supplemental downloadable materials, describe that too. The point of these sections is to convince the publisher that you have a uniquely valuable contribution to offer and that you can deliver the content in a compelling way that readers will find accessible.

Publishers aren't in business just because they love books—they need to be able to sell whatever books they acquire, preferably lots of copies. Therefore, include a section on marketing information to help convince the publisher that this is a good business proposition. Describe any marketing strategies, ways the publisher can position the book to appeal to potential buyers. List the benefits readers would get from it.

Summarize your understanding of the audience profile—the kind of people who would find this book irresistible—and estimate how many of them there are. Don't say, "Every software developer and project manager will want a copy of this book, so the potential market is at least two million copies." First, that isn't going to happen. Second, that doesn't help the publisher position the book in the marketplace.

A key section of the proposal identifies the competitive titles that are already on the market, as well as any that you know are in preparation. For each competitive book, provide the title, author(s), publisher, copyright date, ISBN, page count, price, and a brief abstract. Describe how your book will complement, supplement, and be superior to the competition.

My book proposals include a section on the status of the work. ("The Work" is how the publisher's contract will refer to your book.) The publisher would like to reach a comfort level that you'll actually be able to deliver a usable manuscript on schedule. I know some people who write the entire book before approaching a publisher. I have never done that with my software books, although I did for my nontechnical books. Instead, I outline the book, and then I write a chapter or two to see how it feels and to get a sense for how the whole project might go. At that point I can approach a publisher with confidence that I know what I'm talking about. In this section, I let the publisher know how much I've already written and my estimated schedule for delivering the rest of the content.

Include a section of author information with your full name, contact information, and professional biography. If you've published books previously, list their title, publisher, year of publication, number of pages, ISBN, approximate sales, and any awards they received. Provide references to any articles, handbooks, or e-books you have published. Even if this is your first book, publishers need to know that you can string sentences together.

Along that line, publishers want to see samples of your writing. The general guideline is to submit two chapters that you've drafted, neither of which is Chapter 1. This will give the publisher a sense of your writing style, how effectively you present material, and how much work it will take to massage your manuscript into publishable form. If you haven't written any chapters yet, make sure the publisher has ready access to some of your articles. But if you haven't written any chapters yet, how confident are you that you can write the entire book?

It's no longer the case that you can just write a book and leave everything else to the publisher, cashing the royalty checks as they pour in. Publishers these days are very interested in an author's "platform." Your platform refers to your marketing reach: social media, blogs, discussion groups, presentations and other forums where you can sell books, professional connections, endorsements from people even more famous than yourself. So a section of your proposal should address what *you* will do to publicize, promote, market, and sell your books.

The better known you already are, the happier a publisher will be to see you come along, because it means they can let you bear more of the burden of selling books. If you're not well known yet but have a good idea for a book, you can only hope to find a publisher who's willing to take a risk, so you can then become better known and sell lots of copies of your next book.

It's a vicious cycle that's hard to break into when you don't already have a foot in the door. I have a pretty good platform in the software industry, but I have none at all in the self-help or fiction worlds. This has made it extremely difficult for my nontechnical books in those areas to attract agents, publishers, and buyers, even though they're really good books (trust me). Just be aware of how much promotion work the publisher will want you to do.

The contract

If you succeed in convincing a publisher that your manuscript would be a valuable addition to their lineup, congratulations! You've passed the first hurdle. The publisher will then present you with a lengthy contract that itemizes every aspect of the publishing agreement, more details than you ever imagined possible. Naturally, publishers write these contracts in their own best interest, but you can negotiate some of the terms that might be uncomfortable for you.

I've read—and signed—a number of book contracts, but I am no expert on them and I am not a lawyer. I refer you to Scott Meyers's Advice to Prospective Book Authors web page, http://www.aristeia.com/authorAdvice.html, for some insights on contracting. If you haven't dealt with book contracts before, have an intellectual-property attorney, literary agent, or other expert examine yours for anything you might want to adjust. Here I'll address some of the points I always examine in my contracts.

Author Copies. The first change I always request is in the number of free copies of the book that I'm going to get. The publisher might offer you ten or so copies. But you might need at least thirty or forty copies for your beta readers, family members, early-praise contributors, to send out for post-publication reviews, and to have a few on hand. Don't be shy about asking for more copies. In the scheme of things, that's a tiny expense for the publisher, as they will provide them at their cost, not list price.

Royalties. A contract often expresses royalty rates in terms of two or more tiers. Each tier states the royalty as a percentage of net proceeds received by the publisher—which is far less per copy than the book's retail price suggests—on a certain number of copies sold, less any copies returned by retailers. So you might be offered a three-tier structure something like the following (these numbers are for illustration only):

- Ten percent on the first 5,000 copies
- Thirteen percent on copies 5,001 through 20,000
- Fifteen percent on additional copies sold beyond 20,000

The better your track record of selling previous books, the more leverage you'll have when negotiating royalty rates. Unless you are mega-famous in your field, any royalty percentage above the low twenties is unusual for print books, although you should be able to go higher on e-books.

The contract will include royalty rates for numerous types of sales: domestic U.S., outside the U.S., electronic books, direct sales by the publisher, discount sales, third-party publication (such as licensing the English version to a publisher in another country), translations, site licenses, and so forth. If your book is translated into other languages, you might receive a one-time payment amounting to half the licensing fee for the translation, but you might not receive subsequent per-copy royalties. The contract will spell out all those possibilities, as well as the frequency of royalty payments.

You can negotiate on all of these various royalty percentages and the royalty tier breakpoints if you wish. Just remember that you won't win every negotiation. Win-win negotiation means that everybody walks away feeling like they got at least part of what they wanted and they can live with the compromises they made.

People usually are shocked to learn how little money an author makes per copy of the book. Publishers often discount books by as much as 55 percent for distribution to large retailers. So if your book has a list price of twenty dollars, a retailer might pay as little as nine dollars per copy. Your royalties will be based on the smaller amount, what the publisher actually receives.

By way of example, my most popular software book has sold well for eighteen years. The average list price for the three different editions of the paperback over that time was about $39.00. My royalties average about $2.67 per copy, counting both paperbacks and e-books sold in all formats and markets. Are you surprised? That's just how the traditional publishing business works.

Advances. You can also negotiate on the advance payment, if there is one; not all publishers pay an advance to all authors. An advance is a prepayment against future royalties. Let's say you agree to an advance of $10,000. The publisher might pay you $5,000 upon executing the contract and another $5,000 when you submit the final manuscript. As royalties accrue following publication, the publisher will retain those royalties instead of paying them to you, subtracting the royalties due from the amount you received as an advance. The publisher will begin paying you additional royalties only after they have accrued beyond the amount of the advance.

Don't feel bad if you are not able to negotiate an advance with your publisher. Some publishers simply don't pay them, and publishers don't want to pay more in an advance than they are likely to earn back fairly quickly through sales. I know of one highly respected author of numerous books who has chosen not to accept any advances from his publisher, although I think the publisher would be happy to pay him one. That's certainly your option. Personally, I take the advance.

A friend recently told me about an unusual contract offer she received on a software book proposal from a major publisher. Not only did the publisher not offer her an advance, but the contract required that she purchase all of the copies in a print run herself, presumably to resell or give away on her own. This publisher wanted to transfer much of the financial risk associated with this book to the author, to ensure that the publisher wouldn't be stuck with a lot of unsold copies. That contract clause would have required an upfront investment of several thousand dollars by the author. My friend wisely rejected this skewed contract and was able to place the book with another mainstream publisher, who offered much more reasonable terms.

Reserves. Another point that often requires discussion is the language regarding reserves withheld against returns. Retailers do not always sell all the copies they purchase from a distributor, although royalties from those purchases were already credited to the author. When sellers return unsold copies to the publisher for a refund, those paid royalties need to be subtracted from the author's royalty tally.

The publisher might hold back a certain percentage or an absolute dollar amount of royalties due to the author as a protection against having to claw back royalties previously paid. In most cases the royalties you will accrue from ongoing sales will more than cover the amount lost from returns. However, publishers create this reserve of withheld royalties as a cushion against excessive refunded royalties because of book returns.

Nearly every book contract I've read included a reserve clause like this. However, they often do not explicitly state the mechanism or timing by which the author will ultimately receive the balance of the withheld reserve. Make sure to work out a resolution to the return issue with the publisher during contracting so they can't hang onto your withheld royalties forever or until the book goes out of print, whichever comes first. Once the publisher sees that sales are rolling along at a reasonable clip and returns are modest, you might be able to request to have any remaining reserve amount released to you. I've done this successfully several times.

Copyright. The contract will state who will own the copyright on the book. I like to get the copyright in my own name, not the publisher's name. Maybe this isn't important, but it makes me happy.

Future Books. Some of the contracts I've seen contained a clause that gave the publisher the right of first refusal on my next book. I always ask to remove that clause, as I don't want any restrictions on where I submit future proposals. Who knows what I might write next or where I'll want to send it?

One publisher was especially egregious on this point. They wanted the first option on my next book, but then even if they rejected it and I sold it to another publisher, they wanted to be able to match the offer and get the book. Because the contract does not *require* the publisher to publish the book, they could essentially quash it for a period of time, until we worked out having the rights revert to me so I could try again someplace else. That's all highly unlikely, but there's no way I would agree to those terms.

Responsibilities. The contract will make it clear who is responsible for doing what parts of the work on the project, including who will produce the final artwork, index, and other elements. The publisher will generally hire someone to create the index. I know one author who always generates his own indexes and has persuaded the publisher to pay him for the effort. I've always provided my indexer with a list of suggested index terms, which is usually ignored. This irks me no end. I've never yet been permitted to communicate directly with the indexer for one of my books, which is an ineffective, inefficient, and annoying way to collaborate.

Frankly, some of my invisible indexers did quite a poor job initially, requiring considerable time on my end to get the problems fixed. You have to examine the index carefully to make sure it contains the terms that will help the interested reader find all the goodies contained in the book. This is especially a problem if you're writing highly technical material that even an experienced indexer might not grasp. If the index—or any other aspect of the book—isn't useful or contains errors, the reader is going to blame only you. Remember, your name is on the cover.

Making commitments

Be careful not to commit to a contract until you have a clear idea of where you're going with the book and are confident you can deliver it without killing yourself. One consultant who began writing his opus soon realized he simply didn't have the bandwidth to devote to the book along with his other responsibilities and family life. He was exhausting himself with the effort. Wisely, he decided that the book was a lower priority for him and abandoned it.

Another established author once told me that he was way behind deadline for delivering not just one, but two manuscripts. It wasn't clear that he expected to complete either one, although he had happily cashed the advance checks. If you conclude that you aren't going to deliver the manuscript on time, let the publisher know as soon as possible so they can take appropriate corrective action. This might involve adjusting the schedule, having someone else finish the book, or abandoning the project entirely. The contract should specify what happens under these conditions. And plan to return the advance if you're not going to finish the book.

Staying on track

I have a personal life philosophy to under-commit and over-deliver, which helps me avoid making iffy schedule commitments. This attitude serves me well when I'm working on a book project. It will take longer than you expect to write the book. And simply writing it is just the beginning. I always line up about fifteen friends and colleagues to review the manuscript, chapter by chapter, before the publisher ever sees it. These are my beta readers, as described in Chapter 28, "Four Eyes Are Better Than Two." This adds more time to the process. Besides keeping an eye on the schedule, I'm usually aiming for a book of a particular length, so I need to track the size of the book as well as the status of each chapter as I'm writing. There's a lot to monitor.

To help me stay on top of all this, I set up a status tracking spreadsheet at the beginning of each book project. You can see a sample of one of my book status tracking spreadsheets at https://tinyurl.com/goingitalone. I admit it: I like data. This level of tracking is comfortable for me; it might not make sense for you at all. My spreadsheet contains three sections in separate Excel worksheets: chapter status, review status, and size tracking.

Chapter Status. I list all the book elements I need to create, including chapters, foreword (if any), preface, any introductions to individual parts of the book, appendices, glossary, references, author biography, and so forth. For each element, I record the following dates:

- Drafted
- Sent out to beta readers
- Review comments received
- Baselined
- Submitted to the publisher
- Received after copy editing
- Revised copy returned to the publisher
- Page proofs received
- My page proof comments returned to the publisher
- Comments on final pages returned to the publisher

I establish target dates for major milestones, such as sending out chapters for review and submitting them to the publisher, so I can quickly see whether or not I'm on schedule.

Review Status. For each of my reviewers, I record the date that I received their comments on each chapter. I also make a notation as to how helpful their feedback was, on a scale from 0 to +++. The pattern that results lets me identify the most helpful, reliable, and prompt reviewers. I'll keep them in mind for the next book.

Even though I don't have any trouble getting reviewers to volunteer, I'm astonished at how many of them fail to return any feedback at all. They don't even explain why they aren't commenting on what I send them. They disappear as though they were abducted by space aliens. Weird. If you sign up to be a beta reader but then cannot participate for some reason, please have the courtesy to let the author know as early as possible. He's counting on you.

Size Tracking. I generally target my books for a particular approximate length, based on the story I'm trying to tell and what I think will best fit the market. If you're not doing this, you can skip this section. I estimate the length of each chapter in words, based on my outline. Then I record the actual number of words in the draft version that goes out for review and the final version of each chapter. My spreadsheet calculates the cumulative number of words to date and charts the actual versus expected word count so I can see what the deviation is. Some books have wound up as much as 20 percent longer than I estimated, although I'm getting better at projecting lengths and writing to those targets.

I agree, this is all rather high-resolution, but it helps me get the book done in the way that I'm aiming for. Being a research scientist by background, I'm a data kind of guy, so this is actually fun for me. Peculiar, I know.

Alternatively, you could just start writing your book and stop when you reach the end. Whatever works for you.

Chapter 32

Being Your Own Publisher

Numerous options are available today for authors who wish to publish their books on their own. You might opt for self-publication for several reasons. Perhaps you haven't been able to attract an agent or publisher. Maybe your technical book is targeted at a small niche market or your nontechnical book is a family keepsake, not a commercial endeavor. Perhaps you just don't want to wait the years it can take to submit queries to potential agents and publishers and suffer through countless rejections in hope of eventually getting a hit.

Or maybe you've heard about authors who self-published and scored big, selling tens of thousands of copies of their books and ultimately attracting a traditional publisher that way. Yes, it happens, but don't count on it. According to one source, approximately 1.4 million books were published in the United States in 2013. About three hundred thousand were from traditional publishers, so there's a *lot* of self-publishing going on. A friend who has been in the publishing business for decades told me that the average book published in English in the United States sells somewhat fewer than four copies per year. You're not going to retire early on those royalties.

I've gone the self-publishing route myself a few times. Let me tell you what I've learned.

Self-publishing: Cheap

It used to be that self-publishing a book was essentially an admission of defeat, acknowledging your inability to entice a real publisher.

Today, however, self-publishing is a viable option for many authors. Some authors turn to vanity presses, companies that charge you money to publish your book. They may or may not effectively promote it, distribute, it, sell it, or pay you royalties. Self-publishing and vanity presses aren't the same thing these days.

Yes, going the self-publishing route probably still means that you weren't able to find a traditional publisher. However, numerous tools and options are available, and it is possible—although not a certainty—to achieve commercial success doing it yourself.

I can't describe the self-publishing business in great detail, but I have self-published two books, in addition to this one. The first one was a special situation. When I was a child, my family lived in Europe for three years because my father was in the U.S. Air Force. We did extensive sightseeing throughout Europe. My parents wrote up notebooks about our adventures, complete with photographs, which became treasured family keepsakes. For my mother's eighty-fifth birthday in 2011, my siblings and I decided to publish all of these notebooks together as an actual book titled *You Can't Get There from Here*. That was a catchphrase our family often used as we drove around Europe trying to figure out how to get to some interesting-looking castle or other location we spotted.

You should have seen the expression on Mom's face when we gave her the book. How often does someone present you with a book with your name as the author and you didn't see it coming?

For this self-publishing experience, I used CreateSpace, which is Amazon's self-publishing platform for paperbacks (Kindle Direct Publishing is their platform for publishing Kindle books). It went surprisingly smoothly and was a valuable learning experience for me, in many respects. We did not attempt to sell this book commercially at the time. Of course, that is an option with CreateSpace. You can have your book listed for sale on Amazon.com almost immediately. Just set the price in various currencies, choose the distribution channels you have in mind, and click a button to release your book to the whole world.

These books are printed on demand, so the author need not stockpile—and perhaps ultimately discard—hundreds or thousands of copies from a big press run. With print on demand (POD), when someone orders a copy, the printer manufactures a copy and ships it to the customer. They look like regular books, although you can sometimes spot self-published books because of the minimalist cover design and amateurish interior layout from some do-it-yourselfers. Many brick-and-mortar bookstores will not stock print-on-demand books.

CreateSpace offers a wide range of publishing options. I took the simplest path for my mother's book. I did the copy editing, and then I tackled the cover design ("full cover wrap" = front cover + spine + back cover) and interior design—both new experiences for me—and simply uploaded the resulting PDF files to CreateSpace.com. CreateSpace staff reviewed my files and concluded they would print satisfactorily, so I ordered a proof copy. I made a couple of small corrections in the cover layout, and my sharp-eyed sister spotted several content errors during a final proofread. I uploaded the corrected files, and again they passed scrutiny. I ordered a second proof copy to confirm the changes, and we were done. The entire process cost just $63.34:

- $10.00 for an ISBN, so the book could be published using my own publishing imprint, Agent Q Bookworks, rather than showing CreateSpace as the publisher
- $39.00 as an account upgrade fee that cut the cost of books we purchased approximately in half (CreateSpace has since dropped this option)
- $3.58 plus $3.59 shipping for each of the two proof copies
- My mother's reaction: priceless

This seemed pretty cheap to me. We could purchase all the additional copies we wanted from CreateSpace for just $3.58 each plus the cost of shipping.

So that is one self-publishing extreme, doing everything by yourself. It was a lot of work, but this was a labor of love and, as I said, a great learning experience. I never imagined I would be scanning and retouching eighty-three photographs from fifty years ago.

Self-publishing: Less cheap

At the other end of the spectrum, the self-publishing author who wants to create a truly professional-looking product will hire experts to provide essential services such as copy editing, cover design, interior design, proofreading, and conversion to e-book formats. That's what I chose to do when I wrote my first novel, *The Reconstruction*, in 2017. One of my goals for this project was to never have someone pick up a copy of the book and say, "This looks like it was self-published." Achieving this—and I think we did—required a team effort.

Having never written fiction before, I knew that I had much to learn about writing style. So after I had drafted the manuscript I hired a copy editor who gave me exactly the kind of feedback I was looking for. She helped me correct tenses, suggested when I should replace narrative text with dialogue (or vice versa), prompted me to add more descriptive information about certain characters, corrected some formatting issues, and the like. Laura was very helpful in guiding me to be a better fiction writer.

I also knew I wanted an eye-catching cover that would make people want to learn what this book was about. I mocked up one cover concept as a starting point, but then I hired a professional to take it from there. Vinnie's website displayed a number of appealing covers he had designed for both fiction and nonfiction books. He provided me with several cover concepts, some of which I liked and some of which I did not. It took a number of iterations, with us both contributing ideas and modifications, but eventually we came up with a cover design I really liked. You can see it at http://www.TheReconstructionBook.com. Hiring a professional also ensured that he could create high-quality graphics and properly size the full cover wrap so it would be accepted by the self-publishing platforms I chose to use.

The prices I was quoted for the book's interior design seemed high to me. I decided to give it a shot myself, having had a little bit of experience with that on my mother's book. Her book contained many photos that had to be positioned just right, some maps, and other graphics. My novel was just plain text; how hard could it be?

It turned out not to be terribly difficult to come up with a basic interior design. I went to the library and studied the layout of numerous similar works of fiction that were published in the trade paperback format (as opposed to mass-market paperback or hardcover). I measured margins, took notes on running headers, looked at fonts and their size and spacing, and examined how the first pages of chapters were styled.

Beyond the text of the novel itself, I had to lay out all the front matter and back matter: title page, copyright page, dedication, acknowledgments, and author biography. Some self-publishing platforms will let you download templates for the interior layout once you have selected a trim size (the dimensions of the printed book).

Interior design includes the following activities:

- Set the margins all around each page, mirroring the left (verso) and right (recto) pages, and recognizing that the inside margin needs to be larger on each page to account for the binding.
- Choose the typeface (font), its point size, and leading (pronounced "ledding," the vertical white space between lines) for the basic text.
- Define the typeface, style, and formatting for any special types of text, such as block quotations and chapter titles.
- Define and format running headers and footers.
- Make the first page of each chapter distinctive somehow.
- Define indentation standards that you'll follow. Typically the first paragraph in a chapter and paragraphs immediately following a heading or a scene break within a chapter are flush left, but all other paragraphs are indented. Normal text is fully justified using a proportionally-spaced font.
- Select any highlighting patterns you wish to follow. For instance, I highlighted the first three words of each chapter in *The Reconstruction* using a different typeface, in **BOLD SMALL CAPITALS**, just to provide a bit of distinction.

- Lay out the table of contents and index, if you have them.

The interior design was not horribly complicated, once I decided what I wanted it to look like. However, flowing the text into that template opened a whole new world of knowledge to me about hyphenation rules and layout conventions. Following these sorts of rules can help you make sure your printed book does not look like it was self-published.

As an example, the bottommost lines on facing pairs of left–right pages should align. If you created your manuscript in Microsoft Word and had turned on widow and orphan control to avoid having single lines of text from a paragraph at the bottom (orphans) or top (widows) of the page, you might well have different numbers of lines on some pairs of facing pages. I had to fix all of those manually.

And the hyphenation rules! Do not have an end-of-line hyphen in the first line of a paragraph, the next-to-last line of a paragraph, the last or next-to-last line of a page, or the first line of a new page. Do not have end-of-line hyphenation in an already hyphenated word, a URL, or a word that contains other punctuation, such as an apostrophe. Have at least two or three characters before and after the hyphen in a word that's hyphenated at the end of a line. I also found that Word's automatic hyphenation did not always split words correctly, so I had to fix a few of those errors manually.

Correcting all of these layout issues required numerous passes through the book and a lot of manual tweaking. To follow all the hyphenation rules, I needed to squeeze characters in certain lines closer together so a hyphenated word at the end of the line would wrap upward. In other spots I had to insert manual line breaks to force a hyphenated word down to the next line. Even then, some pages that looked fine in Word didn't look fine in PDF. Very tedious. I mean seriously tedious. Tedious to the max.

Microsoft Word is not the ideal tool for such manipulations. Professional book designers use tools like Adobe InDesign, true desktop publishing software, but I didn't have that available. My book interior came out fine, but it took considerable manual effort.

A valuable resource to help me make my interior layout look as professional as possible was *80 Common Layout Errors to Flag When Proofreading Book Interiors* by Lynette M. Smith. Fortunately, not all eighty of those rules applied to my novel, although they would be relevant to technical and other nonfiction books.

The good news is that if you only plan to publish in e-book form you don't need to worry about all these layout minutiae. The user of an e-reader can change the font, text size, line spacing, and page width so the words do not flow in a predictable way on the page. Such text is in fact called "reflowable." Issues like hyphenation and the fine-tuning of spacing within a line disappear.

Getting people who really know what they're doing to contribute to the project adds to the cost. You need to decide what your budget will bear and how much of the creative work you can do yourself versus hiring experts. Consider whether the investment is likely to pay off in greater sales, helping to get the book picked up eventually by an agent or a traditional publisher, or just personal satisfaction for a job well done.

Here's approximately how the costs broke down for the three hundred pages of *The Reconstruction*:

- Copy editing: $2,640
- Cover design and consulting on self-publishing: $1,500
- Proofreading: $1,050
- Conversions into two e-book formats, MOBI for Kindle devices and readers and EPUB for most other readers: $800
- A package of ten ISBNs plus a barcode with price to put on the back cover of the paperback: $320 (Each book format—paperback, various e-books, audiobook, large print—needs a unique ISBN, although Kindle e-books published through CreateSpace do not. You can buy ISBNs individually or in packages from Bowker Identifier Services at https://www.myidentifiers.com.)
- Licensing images for the cover from Shutterstock.com: $29

- Registering the copyright with the U.S. Copyright Office: $35

Throw in a couple of proof copies and some other odds and ends, and the total price to turn the manuscript for my exciting mystery novel into an actual, high-quality book was about $6,400. That's one hundred times what it cost to self-publish my mother's book, for which I did all the work myself. Not cheap.

Was it worth it? I'll have to sell a lot of copies of *The Reconstruction* to earn back my investment, and that probably won't ever happen. But, hey, I wrote a novel! It was the most fun I've ever had writing. So it was worth it to me to do it right. And it's actually a good read.

Many self-publishing companies offer a range of other services if you're not willing or able to do all these things yourself or to locate and hire professionals who can. You can pay those companies to help with cover and interior design, editing, marketing, promotion, and distribution, in just about any combination, for prices ranging from a few hundred dollars up to several thousand dollars.

I'm not pushing CreateSpace over other self-publishing alternatives. It's simply the one with which I've had the most personal experience. Other self-publishing companies include IngramSpark (which I also used as a printer and distributor for *The Reconstruction*), Lulu, AuthorHouse, Dog Ear, Booklocker, and many more. Smashwords specializes in e-books, as does Amazon's Kindle Direct Publishing. IngramSpark offers the advantage of providing both printed and e-book distribution to many retailers, including brick-and-mortar bookstores, that might not carry books published through CreateSpace.

It can be confusing to try to navigate all the complexities of self-publishing: setting up distribution channels, getting books into all the right formats, choosing prices in various currencies, setting up payment mechanisms, and on and on. I did encounter a few problems during my self-pub journeys. Fortunately, the customer support from both CreateSpace and Smashwords has been first rate, so we solved the problems.

Of course, even having a lovely new paperback available through major book distribution channels is no guarantee that a particular store will elect to stock your book or that customers will buy it.

Self-promotion

No, not telling everyone what a fine human being you are, but rather telling prospective buyers what a great book you've written. Regardless of which self-publishing route you choose, there's one thing that everyone who has self-published agrees on: you must be prepared to promote, promote, promote your book. Some people seem to feel that "If you print it, they will come." It's more accurate to say, "If you print it and tell them about it over and over, they might come." Even if you go with a traditional publisher, plan to spend a lot of your own time and energy on promotion and marketing.

There are many websites devoted to tips for marketing your self-published book. I'll let you pursue those on your own when you're ready. The approach you take for marketing depends somewhat on the genre in which you are writing. Following are just a few suggestions about possible marketing and promotion techniques. Some may work for you; others may not.

- Post announcements on all of your social media outlets, early and periodically. (A caution: I've learned that the numbers of "likes" and nice comments you get about your book on social media do not translate into sales.)
- Join relevant LinkedIn groups before the book appears and begin contributing to discussions to give other visitors the sense that you have something useful to say.
- Post short, but substantive, articles adapted from the book on LinkedIn, and post pointers to it in relevant groups.
- Contact local newspapers to see if anyone is interested in doing a story about you and your book. I've done this successfully for several books.
- Ditto for local television and radio stations.
- Set up an Amazon Author page.

- Ask people with some name recognition to write early-praise blurbs. You can put those on the back cover, on a page just inside the front cover, and in your book description for online retailers, such as the Editorial Reviews category in the Books section of your Amazon Author page.
- Ask anyone to whom you have sent complimentary copies or announcements about the book to post reviews at online retailers. They might need to be reminded a few times.
- Contact libraries and bookstores that might want to stock it. If they can buy it from a large distributor, such as Ingram, that might be more appealing for them than if it's only distributed by CreateSpace.
- Contact websites or magazines about writing articles adapted from the book and possibly reviewing it.
- Contact anyone you know who writes book reviews to see if they will post a review of it. There are websites that will write reviews for money; I've never tried any of them, so I don't know if that is worth the price.

The list could go on and on. Basically, you are trying to override this sad truth I shared earlier about being an independent anything, including consultant or author: "It doesn't matter how good you are if no one knows you're there." I encourage you to search for the numerous websites that offer recommendations for promoting your book. Choose the mechanisms that look like they would be the most effective for your title and the most comfortable for the amount of time and money you wish to invest in promotion.

You can read glowing testimonials from people who sold hundreds of thousands of copies of their self-published book and made a lot of money. The reality, I'm afraid, is that this is highly unlikely to happen with your books—or mine. Sorry. But I wish you the best of luck, and I hope you have fun along the way. I have.

Chapter 33

On Co-Authoring a Book

Several years ago I did something I had never done before: I co-authored a book. It worked out remarkably well. I've written several magazine articles with other people, which went fine, but nothing like the scale of this book. If you've ever thought about writing something collaboratively, you might find the story of how we approached this project informative.

In August of 2012 Joy Beatty, vice-president of research and development at Seilevel, asked me if I had thought about writing a third edition of my popular book *Software Requirements*. The first edition was published in 1999 and the second in 2003, both by Microsoft Press.

I had indeed considered writing a third edition from time to time. Virtually everything I described in the second edition was still valid nine years later, and the book was still a solid seller, but it would benefit from an update in many respects. Important changes had taken place in the software world in the intervening years. Some of the content definitely was ripe for beefing up and could use an improved presentation.

Frankly, though, the prospect of revising a five hundred-page book was daunting. I knew it would be a massive amount of work. I hadn't been following the software requirements literature closely since I had largely retired from consulting and training a few years earlier. The hammock, my guitars, and volunteer work were more appealing to me than spending hundreds of hours at a keyboard yet again. I recognized the need, but I wasn't super-motivated.

Nevertheless, Joy's question got me to thinking. What if she and I were to write the third edition of the book together? Joy was well respected in the business analysis field, up-to-date on current happenings, and the co-author herself of a nice book called *Visual Models for Software Requirements*. We began kicking this possibility around. Before long it became clear that there might be value in this collaboration. We agreed to give it a try.

Requirements for requirements

Our first task was to create an outline. We began with the outline for the second edition, or 2E. We identified chapters that would benefit from major enhancements, chapters that just needed a tune-up, and new topics we could add. We each went through a copy of the 2E and noted specific changes to make. I came up with more than 150 sticky notes with ideas, strategically placed at the relevant sections in the 2E. My email archives contained more than sixty email exchanges I had had with readers over the years (including several with Joy herself from 2004 and 2008) addressing questions they had asked me. Those emails were a rich source of improvement ideas and stories to share.

Joy and I soon settled on the overall chapter structure and our preliminary first- and second-level headings. Then we enhanced this outline, both of us adding bullets under each chapter with our thoughts about possible changes. This annotated outline became our primary working tool for exchanging ideas. In essence, that outline and all the associated notes established the requirements for our book on software requirements.

We incorporated the high-level outline into the proposal we submitted to Microsoft Press. Joy and I were pleased when Microsoft accepted our proposal, as they had done a nice job for us on our previous books.

Across the miles

I live in Portland, Oregon. Joy lives in Austin, Texas. We had only met once in person before we kicked off this project, a year earlier at a conference. We needed to determine the best way to exchange materials throughout this nearly year-long project.

Joy established a Microsoft SharePoint repository for us to use as a configuration management tool. We also set up an issues list to track the myriad questions we knew would arise. We created the following folders in the repository for managing the files:

- A folder containing the final chapter files from the 2E, which served as a great starting point for much of the new book
- A folder for the draft chapters we would be iterating on during initial writing, when making our own revisions, and during peer review
- A folder for the many figures and other images, organized into subfolders for each chapter
- A folder for the submitted chapters that went off to the publisher for copy editing and the edited versions the publisher returned to us
- A folder for PDFs of the final chapter pages we received from the publisher for proofreading
- An infrastructure folder to store our status tracking spreadsheet, chapter checklist, collaboration process, reviewer's guide for our beta readers, the issues list

As each of us uploaded a modified version of a chapter or other document to one of these folders, it was added to the collection so we could retain the history of previous versions. We used check-out and check-in procedures to ensure that only one of us at a time could alter a particular file.

This basic configuration management discipline kept us from overwriting each other's work and losing changes one of us had made. Retaining the earlier versions of each chapter allowed us to go back and see how we had handled some topic before or to repair an error if we accidentally lost some material. It would be a real challenge to execute a project like this without some kind of shared file repository.

Planning the collaboration

I have long suspected that many teams of people who work together on a project don't spend much time thinking about just *how* they're going to work together. They can do fine for a while, but when deadlines loom, there's too much going on, and the stress level ramps up, the lack of a process begins to show. Joy and I invested quite a bit of time working out the process we would follow for our collaboration on the different aspects of this book.

Each of us took primary authorship responsibility for certain chapters. We adjusted that allocation as we went along to share the workload equitably. We crafted a detailed process that described how we would hand materials off from one to the other, address feedback received from our beta readers, and interact with the publisher's editorial team.

We also agreed on some writing style and formatting issues. A key goal was to give the book a consistent feel and style. We did not want it to be apparent to a reader which of us had written a particular chapter. This was perhaps easier when we began with chapters from the 2E. Even on new chapters, though, the numerous passes we made back and forth smoothed out the final presentation into a consistent voice.

Joy and I even discussed how we would resolve conflicts if we held different opinions about a particular issue. My experience has been that in business collaborations it is far better to agree on how to resolve these matters *before* you confront the first conflict, not in the heat of the moment when the parties are emotionally defending their entrenched positions. It was well worth the time we spent working out all these details of our collaboration process.

Tracking status

When writing a large book, there is a vast amount of information to keep track of. At any given time each of our chapters was in one of many possible states:

- Not yet begun
- Initial draft written
- Initial draft being reviewed by the other author
- Reviewed draft being revised by the lead author
- Out for peer review
- Being revised following peer review
- Being edited by our own internal editor
- Submitted to publisher for copy editing
- Being revised following copy editing
- Final manuscript version submitted to publisher
- Formatted PDF pages and artwork received from publisher
- Formatted pages being proofread and corrected
- Corrected pages being proofread yet again
- Final final final pages submitted to publisher (unless, of course, we spot any more errors after that)

Our book contained more than forty components, including thirty-two chapters, front matter (dedications, introduction, acknowledgments), and back matter (epilogue, three appendices, glossary, references, index). There were also more than one hundred image files for figures. We worked on many elements simultaneously in these various states. Sometimes I felt as though I was juggling a dozen flaming chainsaws. We set up a spreadsheet to track the date each chapter transitioned from one of these states to another. Each of us had to maintain our own set of pending revisions to the shared tracking spreadsheet so we wouldn't step on each other's changes when we updated it periodically.

We also established a tracking spreadsheet for review status. We recorded when each chapter went out for peer review, the target date for receiving review feedback, the actual date we received feedback from each reviewer, and a rating of how useful each reviewer's input was. Frequently updating this status tracking file was a bit of a nuisance, but it was part of the necessary process overhead associated with collaboration. Any time multiple people work on an activity there's a certain amount of inefficiency, along with a need for coordination that you simply have to expect and accommodate.

Tracking status like this was essential to make sure that we always knew what each of us should be working on. It helped guarantee that we could achieve our target dates for getting chapters where they needed to be.

Joy and I carefully scheduled those target dates for critical chapter milestones, and then we rescheduled them as we saw how the work progressed. We had a lot of schedule flexibility until the publisher's editorial team was put into place. At that point, they needed firm commitments regarding when they could expect to receive chapters. They also needed predictable turnaround on our review of copyedited chapters and final page proofs. Once the editorial team was assembled, the project switched from being rather open-ended to being time-boxed with firm constraints. I'm pleased to report that we made all of our deadlines.

The result

Writing this book was an interesting and fun experience, as well as being a huge amount of work. Joy was, well, a joy to work with. She closed significant gaps in my own knowledge, and she brought a broad set of personal experiences and stories to share. Fortunately, our fundamental philosophies and perspectives were quite similar. Those minor disagreements that we had were easily worked out through the multitude of emails we exchanged each day and an occasional phone discussion. Neither of us ever got too annoyed with the other or had to exercise a veto.

It was great to have someone to bounce ideas off, to clarify my thinking, to help me choose between possible approaches, to judge whether or not to include a particular topic, and to straighten me out when I was in the weeds. Joy also obtained some input periodically from her colleagues at Seilevel, running small chunks of text past them to test their reaction. This quick, real-world input saved us from ourselves more than once.

You might think that working with a co-author who has responsibility for many of the chapters would save time. That was not my experience. If anything, this book took more effort than if I had done it all myself. That's mainly because each chapter went through more iterations than if only one author had been involved, as Joy and I both revised and polished each chapter.

On the plus side, there were many important benefits from the collaboration. First, I couldn't have done it all myself. Joy had expertise that allowed her to write content that I simply could not. She also took certain chapters that I had written years ago for the second edition and greatly enhanced and updated them.

One of my fellow book authors asked me at the beginning of this project, "How are you going to feel about someone messing with your baby?" I had to set my ego aside whenever Joy shredded my work on an old chapter from the 2E. That was easy to do when I saw how much she could improve it.

In addition, working with a co-author made the material I wrote much better. On my previous books, I just did the best job I could on each draft chapter and sent it out to a dozen or so beta readers. This time, Joy and I carefully went over each other's work before anyone else saw it. We committed acts of unspeakable editorial brutality on each other's writing—respectfully, of course—all toward a positive objective. We were each other's toughest critic.

As a consequence, our ultimate presentation of each topic was far clearer and more thorough than it would have been otherwise. We learned a lot from each other. The quality of the work shows the benefit: *Software Requirements, 3rd Edition* won an Excellence Award from the Society for Technical Communication.

Would I work with a co-author on a book again? It would depend entirely on who the co-author was and what kind of value I thought he or she could bring to complement my own knowledge and experience. I recently met a woman who has written a standard textbook on human sexuality, now in its thirteenth edition. Every three years she and her co-author prepare an updated version. I couldn't imagine having such a long-term partnership, spanning decades and writing the same book over and over again. Admittedly, her topic is more interesting than mine.

I have a far better appreciation now of how to partner with a co-author. The lessons I learned working with Joy Beatty on *Software Requirements, 3rd Edition* would be extremely valuable on a future such project. I wouldn't change much about the way we collaborated, as the results show the value of the process we followed.

That said, I think I will let Joy write the fourth edition herself in another ten years. My hammock awaits.

Bibliography

Block, Peter. 2011. *Flawless Consulting: A Guide to Getting Your Expertise Used*, 3rd Edition. San Francisco: Pfeiffer.

Fisher, Roger, William Ury, and Bruce Patton. 2011. *Getting to Yes: Negotiating Agreement Without Giving In.* New York: Penguin Books.

Katcher, Bruce L., and Adam Snyder. 2010. *An Insider's Guide to Building a Successful Consulting Practice.* New York: AMACOM.

Weinberg, Gerald M. 1985. *The Secrets of Consulting: A Guide to Giving & Getting Advice Successfully.* New York: Dorset House Publishing.

_____. 2002. *More Secrets of Consulting: The Consultant's Tool Kit.* New York: Dorset House Publishing.

_____. 2005. *Weinberg on Writing: The Fieldstone Method.* New York: Dorset House Publishing.

Weiss, Alan. 1998. *Money Talks: How to Make a Million as a Speaker.* New York: McGraw-Hill.

_____. 2016. *Million Dollar Consulting: The Professional's Guide to Growing a Practice*, 5th Edition. New York: McGraw-Hill Education.

Acknowledgments

Consulting by its nature is often a solitary activity. Unless you're working in an actual consulting company, you rarely have a chance to learn by observing others in the course of performing their daily work. I'm grateful to the many other consultants who have shared their wisdom with me over the years through discussions or observation. Some of these people were consultants and trainers we brought in to help when I worked at Kodak, people like Dr. John Alden and Dr. Joyce Statz. Others from whom I've learned much were professional peers, fellow software consultants, trainers, and authors, too numerous to mention. Insights from Norm Kerth, Larry Constantine, and Steve McConnell were especially helpful. If you know me, and if you and I have had such conversations, I thank you!

I'm grateful to the people who contributed original articles to my Consulting Tips & Tricks blog and generously granted me permission to reproduce their articles here. Thanks go to Adriana Beal, Joan Davis, Claudia Dencker, Gary K. Evans, Vicki James, Margaret Meloni, and Jeanette Pigeon. I also appreciate the helpful suggestions offered by Richard Hatheway, Dr. Scott Meyers, and especially Gary Evans. Thanks to Joan Davis for a list of collaboration tools and to Mike Cohn for sharing several of his checklists. These are available at http://tinyurl.com/goingitalone, the web page that accompanies this book.

A very special, heartfelt thank you goes out to my exceptionally patient wife, Chris. Like the partner of any consultant, she ate a lot of meals alone and spent hundreds of quiet evenings in an empty house while I was in who-knows-where, teaching who-knows-what class yet again. I sent her a postcard from each destination. It always said the same thing: "Having a wonderful time in <wherever>. Weather is great, sunny and 80s every day. I spend most of my time at the beach. Wish you were here!" The first card was from Peoria, Illinois, in January. It wasn't sunny and 80s. Chris has quite a collection of postcards now. Without her love, encouragement, and patient support for my various crackpot schemes, none of the events that led to this book would have been possible. Thanks, hon!

About the Author

Karl Wiegers has spent the past twenty years as Principal Consultant with Process Impact, a software development consulting and training company in Happy Valley, Oregon. Previously, he spent eighteen years at Eastman Kodak Company, where he held positions as a photographic research scientist, software developer, software manager, and software process and quality improvement leader. Karl received a PhD in organic chemistry from the University of Illinois.

Karl is the author of the books *Software Requirements*, *More About Software Requirements*, *Practical Project Initiation*, *Peer Reviews in Software*, and *Creating a Software Engineering Culture*. He has also written more than 180 articles on many aspects of software development and management, chemistry, and military history. Karl has served on the Editorial Board for *IEEE Software* magazine and as a contributing editor for *Software Development* magazine.

Karl's most recent book is a mystery novel, *The Reconstruction*. He's also the author of a memoir of life lessons titled *Pearls from Sand: How Small Encounters Lead to Powerful Lessons*.

Several of Karl's books and articles have won awards, including *Software Development* magazine's Productivity Award (*Creating a Software Engineering Culture* and *Software Requirements*) and the Society for Technical Communication's Award of Excellence (*Software Requirements, 3rd Edition*).

You can reach Karl at ProcessImpact.com or KarlWiegers.com.

Index

A

accountant, 81-82
acquisitions editor, 204
active listening, 72
advance, against book royalties, 209-210
affiliate programs, 120-121
agent, literary, 204
agreements
  consulting, 62, 89
  licensing, 89-90
  speaking, 87-89
  written, 52
Amazon, 120, 216, 222, 224
Amazon Associates, 120-121
Amazon Author page, 224
anecdotes, in your writing, 172
answers, easy, 41-44
article
  adapted from book, 140, 224
  opening, 188-189
  proposing, 186
  titling, 187-188
AuthorHouse, 222
authors, advice for, 199-200
author's platform, 207
asynchronous methods, 72

B

backups of presentation, 159
Beal, Adriana, 127
Beatty, Joy, 205, 225-232
beta readers, 176-178, 212, 227
Block, Peter, 19, 233
blogs, writing for, 185-189
body language, 70, 73
bonuses from clients, 57
book
  architecture of, 195
  audience for, 205-206
  chapter status tracking, 213
  competitive marketplace, 201-202
  competitive titles, 206
  cover design, 218
  hooks, 196
  interior design, 218-221
  marketing, 205
  outline, 194, 195, 205, 226
  promoting, 223-224
  proposal, 204-207
  publishing, 199-214
  review status tracking, 213
  royalties, 116, 208-209
  sample chapters, 206
  self-publishing, 215-224
  size tracking, 213-214
  status tracking, 212-214
  structure of, 195
  targeting in the market, 200-202
  themes, 195-196
  titling, 203
book writing, 191-197
  approaches to, 193-194
  discipline in writing, 191
  motivation for, 192-193

treating like a project, 191
Booklocker, 222
Bowker Identifier Services, 221
bundling products and services, 80
business
    liability insurance, 94, 107-108
    policies, 97-105
    property insurance, 108
    rules, 97-105

C

cancellation fee, 62, 88, 90, 92-93
cartoons, 162
certifications, professional, 134-136
chapter status tracking, book, 213
checklists, 37-40
    downloads, 38
    for presenting a public class, 39
    travel, 38
Chicago Manual of Style, The, 179
children and consulting, 32-33
choosing a book publisher, 203-204
citing other publications, 144-145
    fair use and, 146
    versus getting permission, 146
client relations, policies for, 103-105
clients
    becoming friends with, 55-56
    being candid with, 130-131
    bonuses from, 57
    consulting as collaborator with, 25-27
    consulting as expert for, 19-23
    consulting as pair-of-hands for, 23-25
    difficult, 59-64, 65-67
    dream, 55-57
    finding, 16-17
    firing, 61-62
    ideal, 55-57
    lack of communication from, 64
    looking for easy answers, 41-44
    problems with, 59-64
    questionable ethics of, 62
    risks from, 52
    solving problems with, 66-67
    troublesome, 59-64
    turning down work from, 52, 56
    who don't pay you, 59-60
co-authoring a book, 225-232
    benefits of, 230-231
    managing files, 226-227
    planning, 228
    process, 228
    resolving conflicts, 228
    tracking status, 228-230
COBRA, 110
Cohn, Mike, 38-39
collaboration, 42, 47
    long-distance, 74, 228
    planning, 228
    risks from, 52
    tools for, 74
    virtual, 70, 71
collaborator consultant mode, 25-27
commitments
    book, 211-212
    managing, 78
communication
    lack of from clients, 64
    when working remotely, 71-72
company
    name, choosing a, 10
    slogan, 11
    website, 11-12
competition, effect on fees, 79
conferences, speaking at, 13, 139, 140, 159-160
configuration management, for book project, 227
consultant,
    as collaborator, 25-27
    as expert, 19-23
    as legitimate leader, 45-48
    as pair of hands, 23-25
    gaining visibility as, 11-13

marketing yourself as, 16-17
why to become, 29-31
consulting
  agreement, 62, 89
  children and, 32-33
  fees, 78
  impacts of, 22-23
  leaving, 30, 31
  lifestyle, 29-34
  negative impacts of, 30, 32
  off-site, 70, 79, 89
  remote, 69-74, 79, 89
  stresses of, 30, 32-33
  three modes of, 19-27
  versus contracting, 3
  virtual, 74, 89, 97
  while at another job, 2, 30-31
consulting modes
  collaborator, 25-27
  expert, 19-23
  pair-of-hands, 23-25
contract
  book publishing, 207-211
  from client, 91, 93-95
  negotiating, 91-96
contracting
  through another company, 17-18
  versus consulting, 3
copy editing, 178-180, 181, 184, 218
copy editor, 178-179, 181-184
copyright
  book, 210
  fair use and, 145-147
  notice of, 143-144
  registering, 144, 222
  respecting, 162
  violations, 148-150
courseware
  e-learning, 118-119
  licensing, 89-90, 116-118
cover design, book, 218
CreateSpace, 216-217, 221, 222, 224
credit report, 95

criminal background investigation, 95

D

Davis, Joan, 69
DBA, 11, 86
deadline, 79, 159, 187, 212, 230
Dencker, Claudia, 123
developmental editing, 180
difficult clients, 59-64, 65-67
disability income insurance, 111-112
disclaimer, legal, 6, 94, 107, 143
discounting prices, 79, 80, 92
documents, reviewing for clients, 20-21, 56
Dog Ear, 222
doing business as, 11, 86
door prizes, 164
Dorset House Publishing, 180, 194, 199, 203
downloads for this book, 5
  book proposal, 205
  book status tracking spreadsheet, 212
  checklist for presenting a public class, 39
  collaboration tools, 74
  consulting agreements, 89
  courseware licensing agreement, 90
  event planning form, 39
  event tracking form, 39-40
  licensing agreement, courseware, 90
  speaking agreement, 87
  time tracking form, 39
  travel checklists, 38
  URL for, 5
drug test, 91

E

E&O insurance, 94, 108-109

early praise, 193, 224
easy answers, 41-44
e-books, 119, 120, 141, 184, 208, 218, 221
   illegal downloads of, 151
   publishing, 221, 222
editing
   copy, 178-180, 181-184
   developmental, 180
   introduction of errors during, 181
editor
   acquisitions, 204
   copy, 178-179, 181-184
   delighting, 187
   developmental, 180
   unhappiness with, 181
   working with, 181-182
ego, 65-67, 149, 177, 231
EIN, 11
elevator pitch, 202
E-junkie, 119
e-learning courseware, 118-119, 140
employer identification number, 11
errors and omissions insurance, 94, 108-109
estimates, changing, 43
ethics, questionable, 62
Evans, Gary K., 15, 29, 81, 107
expenses
   including in fee, 62, 84, 101-102
   paying your own, 84
expert
   consultant mode, 19-23
   witness, 21

F

facilitation, 72, 73
fair use, 145-147
family
   impact of consulting on, 31-33
   staying in touch with, 32
   working with members of, 33-34

fear of public speaking, 153
fees
   cancellation, 62, 88, 90, 92-93
   consulting, 78
   effect of competition on, 79
   finder's, 63
   for speaking at professional organizations, 103
   licensing, 147
   negotiating, 92
   rescheduling, 88, 90, 92-93
   setting, 77-80, 82-85, 101
   setting based on value, 78, 79, 83
   training, 78
financial
   planner, 86
   policies, 101-103
finder's fee, 63
firing a client, 61-62
Fisher, Roger, 95, 233
formatting book interior, 218-221
forms
   event planning, 39
   event tracking, 39-40
   time tracking, 39
flip charts, 72, 162, 165
frequent flier programs, 100
full cover wrap, 217, 218
future books, 211

G

glossophobia, 153
Goldilocks and the Three Bears, 46
Goodies Collection, Process Impact, 120, 134, 151
guarantee, money-back, 88, 104, 109

H

handbooks, 119, 140
health care insurance, 110-111
health savings account, 111
hooks, for a book, 196

hotel, checking prices on, 101
HSA, 111
humor in presentations, 162
hyphenation rules, 220

I

ideas, generating, 21-22
imprint, publishing, 217
income, passive, 115-121
income taxes, 11
   estimated payments, 82
incorporation, 85-86
independent consulting, 1-2, 10, 18, 127, 133, 139
   company type, 85-86
   downsides of, 26, 30, 60, 82, 117, 123, 224
   failing at, 9-10
   family impact, 31-34
   getting started in, 1-2, 29-31
   insurance for, 107-112
   leaving, 31
   limitations of, 2-3
   personality for, 15, 16
   responsibilities of, 15, 16
   setting rates, 82-85
   why go into, 2, 29-30, 49
indexing, book, 211
Ingram, 224
IngramSpark, 119, 222
insurance, 107-112
   business liability, 94, 107-108
   business property, 108
   client contracts and, 94, 112
   disability income, 111-112
   errors and omissions, 94, 108-109
   health care, 110-111
   life, 109
   negotiating in client contract, 94, 112
   professional liability, 94, 108-109
   professional malpractice, 94, 108-109

intellectual property, 143-152
   leveraging your, 139-142
   licensing, 118
   misappropriation of, 147-152
   ownership of, 141-142, 146
   protecting your, 147-152
   respecting owner's rights, 146
   rights, 141
   sharing ownership of, 56-57
   work for hire, 141, 146
interior design, book, 218-221
interviews, 50, 51, 124-126
invoice, identifying, 6
IP. *See* Intellectual property
ISBN, 206, 217, 221

J

James, Vicki, 49

K

Katcher, Bruce L., 233
Kerth, Norm, 112
keynote presentations, 155
Kindle, 119, 221
Kindle Direct Publishing, 119, 216, 222
Kobo, 119

L

leader
   definition of, 45
   legitimate, 45-48
leadership, 45-48
   ineffective, 46-47
   just right, 47-48
   legitimate, 45-48
   too strong, 47
   too weak, 46-47
   vacuum, 46-47
legitimate leadership, 45-48
   attributes of, 46
licensing

agreement, 89-90
courseware, 89-90, 116-118
fees, 147
intellectual property, 118
life insurance, 109
lifestyle, the consulting, 29-34
limitation of liability, 109
limited liability company, 86
LinkedIn, 9, 223
literary agent, 204
LLC, 86
Lulu, 222

M

magazines
    article length, 186
    article style for, 185-186
    proposing an article for, 186
    working with editor, 181-182, 186-187
    writing for, 185-189
malpractice insurance, professional, 94, 108-109
management pressure, 43
marketing,
    book, 205, 223-224
    your services, 16-17
McConnell, Steve, 171
Meadows, Donella, 129
meetings
    facilitating distributed, 72-73
    virtual, 69-70
Meloni, Margaret, 65
methods, asynchronous, 72
Meyers, Scott, 199-200, 207
Microsoft Press, 203, 225, 226
modes of consulting
    collaborator, 25-27
    expert, 19-23
    pair-of-hands, 23-25
money-back guarantee, 88, 104, 109
mousetrap, selling a better, 4

N

NAH (not applicable here), 22, 24
name, choosing a company, 10
negotiation, 18, 90, 91-96
    based on interests, 95-96
    of intellectual property ownership, 141-142
    on cancellation terms, 92-93
    on fees, 92
    on insurance, 94
    on usage rights, 93
    on video recording, 94
NIH (not invented here), 22, 24
non-billable time, 84
NOOK, 119
Norm Kerth Benefit Fund, 112

O

office expenses, 85
off-site consulting, 70, 79, 89
organizational politics, navigating, 56
outline, book, 194, 195, 205, 226

P

pair-of-hands consulting mode, 23-25
passive income, 115-121
Patton, Bruce, 95, 233
payment
    at time of event, 62, 102
    delayed, 60
    from contractors, 60
    in advance, 60, 62, 102
peer review, 175, 176-178
    status tracking, for a book, 213, 229-230
permission to reuse intellectual property, 146-147
Pigeon, Jeanette, 45
platform, author's, 207

policies
  billing, 60, 62
  business, 97-105
  client relations, 103-105
  financial, 101-103
  traveling, 97-101
politics, navigating organizational, 56
PowerPoint, Microsoft, 37, 156, 159, 166
presentations
  backups of, 159
  giving, 13
  giving with confidence, 153-160
  opening, 161-162
  tricks for giving, 161-166
prices
  discounting, 79, 80, 92
  setting, 77-80, 82-85, 101
print on demand (POD), 216-217
problem clients, 59-64, 65-67
Process Impact, 2, 10-11, 12, 97, 116, 120, 151, 237
  company slogan, 11
  Goodies Collection, 120, 134, 151
products
  bundling with services, 80
  pricing, 78-79
  selling, 120
professional certifications, 134-136
professional liability insurance, 94, 108-109
professional malpractice insurance, 94, 108-109
professional organizations
  fees to speak at, 103, 134
  participating in, 133-136
  speaking at, 13, 133-134
project management, 51
promoting a book, 134, 223-224
proofreading, 182-183, 184
proposal
  book, 204-207
  sample for book, 205
publisher, 116, 141, 144, 150, 179, 180, 184, 199, 200, 202
  acknowledging original when reprinting, 141
  book contract from, 207-211
  choosing for a book, 203-204
  copy editing and, 179
  developmental editing and, 180
  submitting proposal to, 204-207
  working with, 204
publishing
  articles, 185-189
  books, 199-214
  self, 116, 215-224
  to gain visibility, 12

Q

questions, handling during presentation, 156-157, 163
QuickBooks, 82

R

rates, setting, 82-85
readability statistics, 171-172
referring clients to other consultants, 63
reflowable text, 221
remote consulting, 69-74, 79, 89
  risks of, 70-71
rental car, checking prices on, 101
repeat business, getting, 127-131
rescheduling fee, 88, 90, 92-93
reserves, return, 210
retirement, planning for, 86
return reserves, 210
returned books, 210
reusing intellectual property, 141
reviewing documents for clients, 20-21, 56
risks, 31, 43, 47, 56, 130, 207, 210
  from business partners, 52

from clients, 52
from collaborators, 52
of remote consulting, 70-71
of writing, 150
questions to reveal, 53
to clients, 31, 79, 103
royalties
   advance against, 209-210
   book, 116, 208-209
   negotiating, 209
   reserved against returns, 210
   tiers, 208
rules, business, 97-105

S

S Corporation, 85-86
Seilevel, 225, 230
self-publishing, 215-224
   cost of, 217, 220
   why do, 215
self-review of your writing, 175-176
selling
   products, 120
   yourself, 124-126
services, bundling with products, 80
setting prices, 77-80
SharePoint, Microsoft, on book project, 227
size tracking, for a book, 213-214
slogan, company, 11
Smashwords, 119, 222
Snyder, Adam, 233
social media, for promoting books, 207, 223
Social Security number, 11
sole proprietor, 11, 85-86, 94
SOW, 25
speaking
   agreement, 87-89
   at companies, 103

at conferences, 13, 139, 140, 159-160
at professional organizations, 13, 103, 134
for free, 103
tips for confident, 154-160
speech-recognition software, 183-184
spell check, 176
statement of work, 25
statistics, readability, 171-172
status tracking, book, 212-214, 228-230
stresses of consulting, 30, 32-33
style sheet, 182, 183
subcontracting, 60
supplemental materials for this book, 5
systems thinking, 128-129

T

2X/3X rule, 84-85
taxes
   employer ID number, 11
   estimated payments, 82
   income, 11
third-party placement, 17-18
title
   article, 187-188
   book, 203
tools, collaboration, 74
training fees, 78
traveling, 31-32
   frequent flier programs, 100
   policies for, 97-101
troublesome clients, 59-64, 65-67

U

unreasonable people, 42
URL for book materials, 5
Ury, William, 95, 233

INDEX 247

V

value, setting fee based on, 78, 79, 83
vanity press, 216
video recording, 94
virtual collaboration, 70, 71
virtual consulting, 89
virtual meetings, 69-70
vision statement, 25

W

web page for this book, 5
webinars, 118-119, 133-134, 139, 156, 160
website for company, 11-12
websites, writing for, 185-189
Weinberg, Gerald M., 77, 194, 233
Weiss, Alan, 31, 115, 142, 233
why become a consultant, 29-31
win-win outcome, 31, 45, 46, 48, 80, 209
witness, expert, 21
Word, Microsoft, 171, 220
work for hire, 141, 146
workers' compensation insurance, 94
writing
  books, and 191-197
  discipline, 191
  for magazines, blogs, and websites, 185-189
  for publication, 12
  style, 171, 173-174

Y

Y2K, 30

Made in the USA
Middletown, DE
31 January 2018